WHEN SERPENTS SHED THEIR SKINS

WHEN SERPENTS SHED THEIR SKINS

A Revolutionary Journey

JOEL HAWKSLEY

J & Washington Network

Contents

My mother and, my guiding light, Cheryl Ann Ruby.

These poems whisper the stories you first taught me to read. You, with your unwavering patience, unraveled the mysteries of language, gifting me the power to express and understand. Your unwavering belief in education became the foundation on which I built my world.

Though I never shared these verses with you while you walked this earth, I know your spirit lingers within them. You nurtured a love for history, even when the battles of the past left me bewildered. Perhaps it was the Massachusetts air, thick with whispers of revolution, that sparked my later passion for the stories of time.

This collection is a testament to your legacy, Mom. Each poem, a testament to the love of learning you instilled. May these words find a home in your memory, a silent conversation across the years.

With all my love,

I

A Nation's Birth: From Risk to Revolution

A Nation's Birth: From Risk to Revolution

On July the fourth, we celebrate,
But July the second marked the fate,
When Congress voiced in fervent tone,
The colonies would stand alone.

Yet slow the news from Philly went,
Through Boston's streets, the message sent,
And debates in Congress did prolong,
The signing of our freedom song.

John Adams thought July the second,
Would be the day that history reckoned,
But time and talk made the Fourth the date,

For fireworks and festive state.

But behind this joyous celebration,
Lies the tale of our young nation,
Moments when our freedom's thread,
Hung by a hair, by courage led.

Lexington and Concord

Under April's cloak of night,
Paul Revere rode with all his might,
To warn the Minutemen prepared,
For British troops who near declared.

At Lexington, the first shot fired,
Militia met, though some retired,
But at Concord, patriots stood,
Their spirit strong, their aim was good.

The British forced to then retreat,
A rebel force they could not beat,
Thus began the fight for land,
For liberty, they'd make their stand.

Brooklyn Heights

August's sun of seventy-six,
Found Washington in dire fix,
His men outnumbered, trapped in strife,
The British poised to end their life.

With stealth and silence through the night,

Across East River, out of sight,
A fog embraced their secret flight,
And Washington led to safety's light.

Battle of Trenton

By Christmas time, the cause seemed lost,
The Delaware, by ice and frost,
Was crossed by Washington's brave band,
To Trenton's shores, they made their stand.

A Hessian force surprised, subdued,
A victory small, but spirit renewed,
For weary men, it was a sign,
That freedom's fight could still align.

Saratoga's Turning Tide

In autumn's chill of seventy-seven,
Three British forces planned their heaven,
To cut the colonies in twain,
To split their strength, their cause to wane.

Yet Arnold's charge at Saratoga,
Broke Burgoyne's lines, the fate of toga,
Secured the French to join the fray,
A turning point, a brighter day.

Arnold's Treason

But even as victory seemed near,
Benedict Arnold's treachery clear,

A plot to hand West Point away,
Could have doomed our hopeful day.

Yet André caught, the plan laid bare,
Arnold fled in traitor's snare,
A narrow save, a crisis turned,
A nation's hope once more affirmed.

Independence

From Lexington's first bloodied green,
To Saratoga's hopeful scene,
From Brooklyn's fog to Trenton's fight,
Our freedom's path was born of might.

This Fourth of July, we celebrate,
The founders' risks, our nation's fate,
With fireworks, barbecues, and cheer,
We honor those who brought us here.

For freedom won is dearly bought,
By battles fierce and courage wrought,
A fragile thing, our liberty,
Preserved by those who dared to be.

In moments dark, when hope seemed thin,
When victory was far from kin,
The spirit of a new-born land,
Held firm, and freedom took its stand.

2

On the Cold, Icy Morning
of March 5, 1770

On the Cold, Icy Morning of March 5, 1770

I sing of a dawn, chill and biting, the streets of Boston glistening
With the frost of early March, the breath of the city hanging
In the crisp morning air. The hour, just past nine, on King Street,
Where history stands on the precipice of conflict.

See there, a solitary sentinel, Private Hugh White,
A figure clad in red, guarding the Boston Custom House,
The air heavy with tension, the murmurs of the town,
A wigmaker's apprentice, Edward Garrick, his voice a spark.

Garrick's words, a careless utterance, a challenge to honor,
Captain Goldfinch, accused of debt unpaid, a lie soon revealed,
White, the soldier, his heart aflame, defending his captain's name,

A clash of words, a flash of musket, the apprentice struck down.

Behold, the scene unfolds, passersby draw near,
A trickle turns to torrent, fifty men and boys,
Gathering like storm clouds, their taunts the thunder,
White, retreating to the Custom House steps, his fear a beacon.

The bells toll, iron tongues calling the city's pulse,
The streets awaken, footsteps rushing, a tide of humanity,
Three hundred strong, four hundred, a sea of faces,
Drawn by the commotion, the rising swell of anger.

Captain Preston, within the Main Guard, pacing the floor,
Thirty minutes of indecision, then resolve hardens,
Seven soldiers summoned, bayonets fixed, a corporal's command,
Stepping into the fray, the captain's sword gleaming.

"Lobsters!" "Bloody backs!" the crowd jeers, voices like stones,
Ice, shells, snowballs hurled, a tempest of scorn,
Montgomery falls, a club to the head, a trigger pulled,
The crack of musket fire, the scream of the fallen.

Chaos, blood upon the snow, a heartbeat of violence,
Five souls depart: Attucks, Caldwell, Carr, Gray, Maverick,
Their names whispered in the wind, martyrs of the cause,
Their sacrifice, the ember of revolution's flame.

Governor Hutchinson, his voice a balm, promising justice,
"Let the law have its course," he pleads, the crowd disperses,
Soldiers and captain, arrested, the weight of murder's charge,
The city waits, a breath held, the trials postponed.

Two hundred eyes witnessed, each tale a shard of truth,
The massacre, a symbol, the seed of independence sown,
Captain Preston, in his cell, a letter penned in gratitude,
A plea for fairness, justice over the rabble's wrath.

Months pass, the trials loom, tensions simmer still,
Preston and his men, before the bar, the law's stern gaze,
John Adams, young and resolute, defender of the damned,
His voice, a beacon of reason, in the tumultuous sea.

The British troops withdraw, the city's heart scarred,
But in the echo of musket fire, the cry of liberty,
Boston stands resolute, the path to freedom clear,
A new dawn rises, born of blood and resolve.

3

The Trial of Captain Thomas Preston

The Trial of Captain Thomas Preston

In the autumn's embrace, October's end,
The courthouse stands, a solemn edifice,
A crucible where justice shall be forged,
And Captain Preston, a figure stark and grave,
Awaits the judgment of his peers, his fate entwined
With history's unyielding thread.

Six days unfold, a saga of law and order,
From October's twenty-fourth to twenty-ninth,
A trial long in colonial times,
The jury sequestered, kept from hearth and home,
In service to a higher call, a quest for truth.

John Adams, steadfast, joined by Quincy and Auchmuty,
Stand defenders of the accused, against the tide
Of anger, grief, and blood-stained snow.
Preston, silent by decree, his voice withheld,
Yet his presence, a testament to duty's burden.

A sword drawn, not fired, yet charged with murder's weight,
For as officer in charge, he bears the yoke
Of actions wrought by those under command.
His words, preserved in testimony's breath,
"I did not give the order, I bid them hold."

The jury, cloistered, deliberates the night,
Their minds a battleground of fact and doubt,
Three hours they ponder, then await the dawn,
For justice must be served with measured hand.

October thirtieth, the verdict clear,
Not guilty, for the order was not proved,
A sigh, a breath, a moment's respite gained,
For Captain Preston, freedom's light restored.

Yet the shadow lingers, for Adams knows,
The soldiers' trial, a month hence, draws near,
A heavier mantle to shoulder, a graver charge,
For bloodshed speaks in tongues of fire and fear.

November's chill, the gavel falls again,
Eight men stand accused, the courtroom hushed,
From twenty-seventh's dawn to December fifth,
The trial long, the stakes, a nation's heart.

Through days of witness, argument, and plea,
Adams, a beacon of reason, stands,
Against the fervor, the cry for vengeance sweet,
He speaks of law, of justice's sacred trust.

And as the soldiers' fate is weighed and judged,
A verdict rendered in December's early breath,
History marks these trials, a testament
To a nation's fledgling steps towards liberty.

4

The Courtroom's Song

The Courtroom's Song

In the courtroom's sacred space,
Where lives and fates entwine,
The echoes of our struggle trace,
A future we define.

From Preston's trial to soldiers' stand,
The seeds of freedom sown,
In justice's light, a fledgling land,
Finds courage to be known.

With Adams' voice, with truth as guide,
Through tumult and through strife,
A nation's heart, with law allied,
Begins its quest for life.

In the Courtroom, Autumn's Breath

Upon the crisp air of November,
In the halls where justice reigns,
Eight men stand accused, the specter of guilt
Looming like the frost of early dawn.

Adams, with Quincy and Blowers beside,
A trio against the tide of wrath,
Defenders of those marked by red,
Their task a monumental shield.

Eighty voices rise, witnesses to chaos,
Their tales woven in the fabric of strife,
Adams, a beacon, his words a blade,
Cutting through the fog of vengeance.

Beccaria's wisdom, a guiding star,
"If, by supporting the rights of mankind,"
He begins, the courtroom hushed,
"For invincible truth, I stand alone."

Innocence must be shielded, he declares,
Even at the cost of scorn and loss,
For better that the guilty walk free,
Than one pure soul be unjustly damned.

Preston's trial, a shadow cast,
No order given, no command to fire,
Adams weaves this truth, a cloak,
Against the fury of the crowd.

The soldiers, mere men in a storm,
Adams paints their fear, their desperate plea,
To hold the line, to guard their lives,
In a city that seethes with unrest.

"Facts are stubborn things," he cries,
And passion cannot sway the scales,
The mob's taunts, the missiles thrown,
A tempest in the night, a harrowing gale.

Montgomery struck, the call to fire,
Not malice, but survival's cry,
Witnesses speak, their truths a shield,
Against the charge of murder's lie.

In the midst of turmoil, Carr's last breath,
A voice from beyond, through his healer's lips,
He saw no malice in their eyes,
Only men, cornered, forced to defend.

Two hours, and a half more pass,
The jury's minds a furnace bright,
They find the six not guilty, free,
Montgomery and White, manslaughter's plight.

The brand upon their hands to mark,
A mercy in the law's firm grasp,
For first offense, they bear the scar,
But freedom's breath, they too shall clasp.

Adams, his duty done, stands alone,
The crowd's anger a chilling wind,

Half his practice gone, yet he stands,
A pillar of truth, in liberty's name.

5

Reflection in Solitude

Reflection in Solitude

In the quiet of the night,
Adams ponders justice's light,
The cost of truth, a heavy toll,
Yet in his heart, a whisper bold.

For in defending those despised,
He glimpsed the dawn of freedom's rise,
A nation's heart begins to beat,
In every word, in every plea.

Let history judge with kinder eyes,
The trials where our path was forged,
In autumn's breath, in winter's chill,
The seeds of liberty were sown.

6

December Trial Told

December Trial Told

In the heart of winter, the courthouse stands,
Amidst the frost and colonial snow,
Eight soldiers, redcoats, take the stand,
The echoes of a troubled year aglow.

December's chill wraps the streets of Boston,
Where Adams, Quincy, Blowers stood tall,
Defending those the town had lost in,
March's bloody call, the curtain's fall.

John Adams, firm in icy resolve,
Faces the jury, sequestered and stern,
No Bostonian eyes, to dissolve,
The law's grip, its steady turn.

Eighty voices rise, their truths unfold,
Adams weaves the story clear,
Self-defense in that night so cold,
The soldiers' fear, the crowd's jeer.

"Facts are stubborn things," he declares,
Against the tempest of passions' sway,
The law must stand, amidst all glares,
In truth's light, the facts must stay.

Through his words, the case laid bare,
No order to fire, no malice found,
Montgomery struck, the soldiers' scare,
In self-defense, their actions bound.

Innocence must be protected, he spoke,
More than guilt pursued and met,
A community's core, its very cloak,
In justice's name, their fears beset.

Adams stands, a beacon bright,
His heart aligned with duty's claim,
Against the darkness of mob's night,
His wife's tears, his soul's flame.

On March's third year anniversary,
He reflects on labor and anxiety faced,
Abigail's support, in uncertainty,
Their trust in Providence firmly placed.

"No pride in action," Adams asserts,
Just duty done, in winter's grasp,

To stain the land with unjust spurts,
Would be to break justice's clasp.

A trial not for fame, but for law's heart,
In December's chill, a nation's test,
To show the world, a new start,
Where every soul, by law, is blessed.

The trial's end, a verdict just,
Six acquitted, two lesser blame,
The rule of law, a sacred trust,
In winter's snow, they carved a name.

Boston calm, until tea's bitter taste,
December's party, a different fight,
But in 1770's winter, embraced,
The seeds of law, set firm and right.

Adams, in years hence, would say,
"Gallant, manly, my finest deed,"
In service to country, in winter's fray,
The birth of justice, planted seed.

7

The Hollow Night of December 16, 1773

The Hollow Night of December 16, 1773

In the shadow of ancient wharves,
Where the sea whispers forgotten tales,
The ghost of commerce lingers,
Tethered to the moorings of despair.

Seven thousand strong, a murmuring tide,
From towns twenty miles and more,
Gathered in the twilight of grievance,
Their voices a bitter wind.

The ships, silent and waiting,
Dartmouth and Eleanor, Beaver too,
Cradled the East's delicate leaves,

Secrets of empire's overreach.

Through the fog of discontent,
Figures moved with spectral grace,
Mohawk masks, a defiant guise,
A charade against tyranny's face.

O Griffin's Wharf, where resolve ignited,
Aboard the creaking vessels' planks,
The chests, three hundred forty-two,
Met the cold embrace of the harbor's depths.

Without injury, without flame,
Only the tea, the Empire's gold,
Swirling in the black water,
Symbols of a fraying control.

The night a hollow stage,
Where history's actors played their part,
In the silence of the dawn,
Echoes of defiance lingered.

The sea, an indifferent witness,
Swallowed the leaves' protest,
As Bostonians, shadows on the shore,
Breathed the air of rebellion's birth.

For a decade of abuses,
The evening spoke in volumes,
And the tea, in its descent,
Marked the point of no return.

Thus, the harbor claimed its share,
Of an empire's overreach,
And in the quiet aftermath,
The seeds of revolution stirred.

We, who are hollow men,
Watch from the edge of time,
This act, a prelude to the end,
Of the old world's tarnished rhyme.

In the heart of December's night,
The die was cast in the harbor's gloom,
And the whispers of that restless sea,
Foretold a nation's looming dawn.

8

The Burden of Victory

The Burden of Victory

The war drums ceased, and victory proclaimed,
Yet, beneath the cheers, a burden unnamed.
The Crown, deep in debt from the battle won,
Turned its gaze to the colonies under the sun.

In the distant halls where power resides,
No voice for the colonists, no one to chide.
Scotland, Wales, and England, reluctant to pay,
Looked across the sea, deciding their way.

For seven years, the land had bled,
Fields of green where dreams had fled.
Homes were razed, lives undone,
By the conflict's toll, by the blazing gun.

Now, Parliament's pen with a heavy stroke,
Inscribed new chains, though no words were spoke.
Tax the goods, tax the life,
Of those who bore the brunt of strife.

The Sugar Act, a bitter decree,
For trade bound tight by royal fee.
No goods from lands beyond the Crown,
Only from Britain, the rule laid down.

Sugar, indigo, coffee too,
Each a symbol of what they knew.
Wrought silk, calico, foreign wine,
All ensnared in the Parliament's line.

A mother's love turned to greed,
Ignoring the colony's desperate need.
Protection, defense, a hollow claim,
For revenue's sake, their lives in flame.

Yet from this yoke, a spirit grew,
A whisper first, then a cry anew.
No representation, no rightful voice,
But in their hearts, they made a choice.

The burden placed on weary backs,
Sparked a fire along the tracks.
A nation's birth in whispered breath,
A fight for freedom, a struggle 'til death.

For though the Crown sought to bind,
The human spirit's hard to blind.

In fields once drenched in sorrow's tears,
Rose the courage to face their fears.

And in the end, it was not gold,
But liberty's light that they did hold.
From every act, from every pain,
The dream of freedom began its reign.

So here we stand, on freedom's shore,
Remembering those who came before.
Their burdens borne, their voices strong,
In the silent march, a justice song.

The Bond of Tyranny

The Bond of Tyranny

In the courts of Nova Scotia, far from home,
Where justice bends to wealth and Rome,
The Sugar Act, a chain and yoke,
Around the neck of freedom spoke.

An Admiralty's greed laid bare,
Five percent the judge's share.
Incentive to the Crown's decree,
A mockery of liberty.

To travel north, at heavy cost,
With hopes of fairness surely lost.
A trial in bias, hope turned grey,
No justice found in such a way.

Outrage brewed in merchant hearts,
In homes where freedom's journey starts.
A tax without a voice to speak,
A levy laid upon the meek.

Illicit trade, a rebel's path,
In shadows cast by tyranny's wrath.
To craft and trade by candle's light,
To stand against the taxing blight.

The Crown's grasp tightens, levy by levy,
As colonists grow more unsteady.
"If trade is taxed, then why not more?"
The cry of freedom's roar.

"Why not our lands, our fields so green?
Our every thought, our every dream?"
Boston's voice in meeting's call,
Against the rising tyrant's wall.

For without a say, without a vote,
In laws that press upon our throat,
Are we not slaves in freedom's guise?
With liberty a fading prize?

Use your power, hold the line,
Against this theft, this grand design.
For if we bend, if we give way,
The dawn of freedom fades to grey.

In every hearth, in every hand,
The spirit of a restless land.

To fight the bond, to break the chain,
To see the light of freedom's gain.

The Sugar Act, a spark, a flame,
In hearts that history cannot tame.
From every tax, from every wrong,
Rises the voice of freedom strong.

For colonial call, transcendent voice,
In nature's law, we find our choice.
To stand against the tyrant's game,
To claim our right, to stake our claim.

The soul of man, in freedom's fight,
Against the dark, against the night.
In unity, our strength we find,
A bond unbroken, intertwined.

So let the tyrant's power fall,
Against the might of freedom's call.
In every heart, in every land,
We rise, we fight, we make our stand.

10

The Burden of the New World

The Burden of the New World

In the fading light of the empire's day,
Where the forests whisper secrets old,
The Crown, heavy with the weight of distant wars,
Seeks to bind the frontier with ink and seal.

Pontiac's shadow stretches long,
A rebellion's cry in the wilderness,
Where the Ohio's bloodied waters speak
Of promises broken and dreams deferred.

Across the seas, in halls of stone,
The Parliament debates the fate
Of those who till the rocky soil,

Who carve their lives from the bone of the land.

The Stamp Act, a decree of paper and wax,
Falls like a hammer on the hearts of men.
Every license, every deed, a token
Of the burden laid upon the New World's shoulders.

The Britons grumble in their ancient streets,
Their cobblestones worn with the march of time.
"Why should we pay," they ask, "for battles
Fought in forests we shall never see?"

The Commons, dutiful and loyal, decree,
A litany of levies, a cascade of coins,
For every parchment, every vellum,
A tax to bind the colonies tighter.

In the colonies, the murmur grows,
A river's roar against the dam.
For every card, every dice,
Every sheet of news and tale,
The weight of the Crown presses down.

The ink of law spreads like a stain,
A darkening of the horizon's hope.
In taverns and meeting halls, the fire kindles,
A flicker of defiance in the eyes of men.

The burden of the New World,
A yoke unseen but felt in every breath,
A weight that drives the plow deeper,
That sows the seeds of rebellion and strife.

In the whispers of the pines,
In the rustle of the leaves,
The spirits of the land speak
Of a future forged in the furnace of resistance.

For every stamp, a spark is struck,
A flame that will not be quenched.
The cry of freedom, distant yet clear,
Echoes in the hearts of those who dare.

The Stamp Act, a symbol of the divide,
A line drawn in the sand of time.
In the shadows of the frontier,
A storm brews, a reckoning comes.

The Old World's grasp tightens,
But the New World's spirit rises.
A clash of wills, a test of resolve,
In the crucible of the colonies' fight for life.

In the heart of the wilderness,
In the soul of the oppressed,
The seeds of revolution take root,
Nurtured by the blood of the past,
Watered by the tears of the present,
Growing towards a future of liberty.

I I

The Intolerable Acts

The Intolerable Acts

In halls of stone, across the distant sea,
The Crown, with iron hand, decrees anew,
A clutch of laws to bind the restless free,
To quell the spirit that from rebellion grew.

The Boston harbor, silent in its wrath,
Bears witness to the tea, cast to the tide,
A gesture bold that sealed a perilous path,
And stirred the anger of an empire's pride.

King George, with counsel from his steadfast North,
Commands the yoke be tightened on the land,
"The die is cast," his proclamation forth,
Submit or triumph, by his stern demand.

From March's chill to September's golden glow,
The Coercive Acts, a chain on liberty,
To force the hand of those who dared to show,
Defiance in the face of tyranny.

Yet voices rose, among the English peers,
In Parliament, a murmur of dissent,
With Burke, who warned of consequences fierce,
That such harsh rule would breed a fierce lament.

He saw within the hearts of distant kin,
A fire that punishment could not subdue,
A fierce resolve that tyranny would win,
A spirit bold, to principles most true.

The Crown's design, a vice upon the land,
Sought submission, yet it planted seeds,
Of unity, a stronger, firmer stand,
Against the acts that answered selfish needs.

Intolerable, named by those oppressed,
A litany of laws that choked the free,
Each measure passed, a liberty suppressed,
Each act a call to rally, to decree.

And so, the colonies, in common cause,
Found strength within their shared adversity,
For every act imposed, each grievous clause,
A step towards a bold new destiny.

In fields of green, where Concord's river flows,
Where Lexington would hear the first defiance,

The echoes of these acts, the anger sows,
A shot rings out, the start of their alliance.

For in the hearts of those who cherish right,
The Crown's decrees but kindle freedom's flame,
Through trials harsh, emerges from the night,
A nation forged in liberty's proud name.

Thus, from the edicts meant to bind and break,
A stronger spirit of rebellion stirred,
The Intolerable Acts, a fierce mistake,
For liberty, by their oppression, spurred.

12

Confidence Gained at Bunker Hill

Confidence Gained at Bunker Hill

The sun rose over Charlestown, gold and severe,
Reflecting off the bay like a mirror to fate,
Militiamen huddled in the dawn's cold clear,
Ready to carve their place, beyond the gate.

They moved to Breed's Hill, silent, resolute,
Building a redoubt, their hands the tools of war,
A polygon of hope, in soil firm and mute,
Their eyes cast toward the harbor, to the fore.

Gage watched from Boston, his soldiers poised to sail,
In red coats bright, the empire's might arrayed,
He saw defiance, and knew he could not fail,

A demonstration of force, a decision made.

June seventeenth, an afternoon of fire,
Three thousand strong, the British troops advanced,
With ranks precise, their purpose to aspire,
To crush the rebel spirit, left entranced.

"Don't fire until you see the whites of their eyes,"
Prescott's voice, a whisper, then a call,
To hold, to wait, beneath the summer skies,
To strike with iron resolve, to stand or fall.

The redoubt roared, musket balls in flight,
British soldiers fell, a tide of red retreat,
The ground they sought, now a pyre of fight,
Sheep in a fold, laid down in death's defeat.

Three times they charged, three times they met the flame,
Until the hill, blood-soaked, was finally won,
But at a price, a hollow victor's claim,
For every life, a shadow on the sun.

Pitcairn fell, a symbol of the toll,
A thousand lost, the British paid the price,
While Patriots, with half their number whole,
Found strength in what was lost, a sacrifice.

They did not win, but neither did they break,
From Bunker Hill, a message to the crown,
America would fight, for freedom's sake,
With grit and will, they'd tear the old world down.

The monument stands, a testament of stone,
To those who stood, in dawn's first fragile light,
A fledgling nation, now fully grown,
Forged in the fire of that historic fight.

In the fields of green, where blood once did spill,
The echoes of their valor still remain,
A hill of history, where hearts grew still,
Yet rose anew, defiant through the pain.

Bunker Hill, a chapter etched in time,
Where courage met the empire's wrathful might,
A seed of freedom, planted in its prime,
A dawn of hope, born from the darkest night.

13

Faces of the Battle of Bunker Hill

Faces of the Battle of Bunker Hill

1. **Israel Putnam**

"Old Put" from Connecticut, plowing fields,
news from Lexington, his furrow left behind,
rode a hundred miles to Cambridge, steel
in his heart, the call of battle in his mind.
Once a soldier of the crown, now turned,
his experience both blade and shield,
the redoubt rose under his command, spurned
by a past, now recast in freedom's field.

I. William Prescott

Prescott from Groton, a colonel in command,
saw the high ground, Breed's Hill to defend,
"Don't fire until you see the whites," his hand
steady, his men's courage a message to send.
Erecting fortifications, the twilight's toil,
his words a legend, though sources may debate,
defending New York after, loyal to the soil,
till the war's end, his story and fate.

III. Dr. Joseph Warren

Warren, the doctor, orator of the cause,
his voice in Boston a beacon, bold and bright,
Mason, Son of Liberty, his words the laws
of rebellion, leading through the night.
The Suffolk Resolves, his pen the sword,
a Major General's rank, a soldier's end,
in battle's thick, his life underscored,
by Revere, identified, his body to mend.

I. Major-General John Stark

Stark from New Hampshire, the call to arms,
mustered his men, a regiment's might,
fortified the low ground, prepared for harms,
covering Prescott's retreat in the fight.
Stone fortifications, the Mystic's flank,

a defense both strategic and bold,
his command a bulwark, the enemy to stank,
a leader in the annals of stories told.

I. General William Howe

Howe, the British commander, Boston's siege,
the cost of victory, a burden to bear,
"a success too dearly bought," his grief a liege,
confidence shaken, criticism's snare.
The war's weight upon him, decisions fraught,
a campaign led by doubts and ghosts,
victory's bitter taste, a Pyrrhic thought,
the scorn of the army, and home's posts.

I. General Robert Pigot

Pigot, valorous, Britain's left flank led,
Breed's Hill seized, his bravery marked,
a promotion to colonel, his name widespread,
a victory claimed, the British embarked.
Decisive action in battle's heat,
his commands a key to their success,
yet the price of conquest, lives replete,
a victory's cost, history to assess.

VII. Major John Pitcairn

Pitcairn, the Scot, led the advance,
at Lexington and Concord, his valor shown,
respected by all, in Boston's stance,
early wounded, yet courage grown.
Through rebel trenches, up the hill,
four bullets struck, fell into his son's embrace,
his men wept openly, grief a chill,
hours later, he passed, history's trace.

Epilogue

A monument stands, the stories of these men,
etched in stone, in valor's timeless light,
each face a facet, in freedom's pen,
each life a testament to the fight.
Bunker Hill, where courage met the crown,
a fledgling nation, confidence found,
the echoes of the battle, in history's gown,
a cry for liberty, forever unbound.

14

The Midnight Artisan

The Midnight Artisan

In Boston town, where shadows creep,
And whispers of rebellion seep,
A man of metal, mold, and might,
Paul Revere, in darkest night.

With copper plates and chisel keen,
He carved the truth, though seldom seen,
By tyrants' eyes, the tales unfurled,
Of Boston's plight to wake the world.

His engravings, fierce and raw,
Showed oppression's iron claw,
The massacre, the blood-stained street,
Where freedom's ghost and courage meet.

In midnight's cloak, on hooves of steel,
He rode to break the tyrant's wheel,
"By land or sea," the lanterns gleamed,
A signal bright, the patriots dreamed.

"One if by land, and two if by sea,"
His message flew, his heart's decree,
To warn of redcoats' stealthy tread,
The dawn of liberty ahead.

Through Lexington, through Concord's vale,
His cry resounded, strong and hale,
"Awake! Awake! The hour is nigh!"
Beneath the spangled, starry sky.

Old North Church, your bells rang clear,
Paul Revere, we hold you dear,
Not just for ride, but craft and skill,
The artisan with iron will.

In workshops dim, where fires burned,
His foundry forged, his spirit yearned,
To build a nation, strong and free,
From Boston's heart, to shining sea.

In twilight's gloom, his legacy,
A testament to liberty,
With every bell, and every chime,
A pulse of freedom through all time.

So let the records show and tell,
Of Revere's ride, and midnight spell,

Yet more than that, the craftsman's hand,
Which shaped the destiny of our land.

15

Franklin's dedication to public service

Franklin's dedication to public service

In the quiet of his mind, experiments did spark,
Yet his heart sought the people's call, a journey to embark.
A gentleman of leisure, but not of idle dreams,
He served in councils, halls of peace, where justice softly gleams.

In Philadelphia's heart, he rose, a leader born anew,
In '48 the council called, in '49 justice too.
By '51 an alderman, assembly's voice he found,
Yet his eyes were on a realm where larger hopes abound.

The British Empire's structure, a marvel to his gaze,
In '53, a post he held, through northern lands' long days.
Intercolonial visions grew, a Plan of Union drawn,

But unity was far from reach, its time had yet to dawn.

To England then, in '57, he sailed with fervent plea,
For Pennsylvania's voice to rise, for fairer taxes free.
Yet larger schemes did fill his heart, to royal provinces lean,
In London's grand, expansive arms, his influence was seen.

From famous minds to royal halls, his name in reverence spoke,
Degrees of honor graced his life, as portraits gently woke.
A love for England's polished ways, a contrast stark and bright,
Yet America's simpler soul remained his guiding light.

Through storm of Stamp Act's heavy hand, his loyalty did strain,
A firestorm in the colonies, where freedom called in pain.
In Parliament he stood his ground, his words a nation's shield,
A wisdom born of service true, no power would he yield.

Between two worlds he walked with grace, an envoy of the time,
His pen a bridge, his heart a link, in prose and purpose prime.
Yet in the tumult of the day, his "Americanness" grew clear,
A future free, a destiny, to which he held so dear.

In France, a court of elegance, he donned a simple guise,
For in his heart he carried dreams of liberty's sunrise.
An architect of treaties bold, through years of pain and strife,
He shaped a world, a story told, in the twilight of his life.

Oh, Benjamin, a soul so vast, who served with heart and hand,
From city streets to royal courts, he heeded freedom's stand.
In science, service, wisdom's light, his legacy unfurled,
A testament to human might, a beacon to the world.

16

The Rising Storm

The Rising Storm

The drums of war beat far and wide, across the wild frontier,
The French and Indian strife did call, new lands to British cheer.
Yet victory's crown, though splendid worn, weighed heavy on the throne,
For taxes steep and burdens sore, the seeds of strife had sown.

Oh colonies, vast and vibrant, under Albion's grasp so tight,
Your voices raised in protest bold, for liberty and right.
The Stamp Act's ink, a tyrant's mark, the Townshend's grip so cold,
In Boston's streets, in fervent hearts, resistance fierce and bold.

A massacre on winter's night, where five brave souls did fall,
The mob's outcry, the soldiers' fire, a cry for justice all.
And in the harbor's moonlit glow, the tea did darkly spill,

A tempest in a teapot's storm, a clash of iron will.

The Coercive Acts, intolerable chains, sought to bend the free,
But in Philadelphia's hallowed halls, the call to unity.
From Virginia's fields, Washington came, Adams' fiery word,
Patrick Henry's voice, with liberty's flame, in every heart was stirred.

Not yet a call for severed ties, but rights as subjects claim,
Representation in the halls, equality's fair name.
A declaration bold and true, of rights all men should hold,
Life and liberty, property's due, assembly's freedom bold.

April's night, the lanterns lit, Revere's swift ride began,
Through Concord's fields, Lexington's green, the militia made their stand.
The redcoats came, the muskets roared, a nation's dawn did break,
"The shot heard round the world" did roar, a new path to take.

For every man, a voice to raise, in union's strength and pride,
The Revolutionary fire ablaze, with justice as its guide.

17

The Spirit of Rebellion

The Spirit of Rebellion

I sing of conflict, the birth pangs of a nation,
From far-flung forests and rivers wide, the crown's grasp extended,
The French and Indian War, a stage set for greater acts,
New territories won, yet debts deepened, the crown's coffers drained.

Oh colonies, spirited and restless, feel the tightening yoke,
Stamp Act, Townshend Acts, Tea Act—arbitrary and unjust,
From the Atlantic's edge, a cry rises, "No taxation without representation!"
A people unbowed, demanding their ancient rights.

In Boston's streets, tensions flare, soldiers and townsfolk clash,
A massacre in cold blood, five souls martyred for the cause,

Their blood stains the cobblestones, a rallying cry for freedom's march,
From the harbor, the tea is cast—342 chests, a defiant brew.

Parliament's response, swift and harsh, the Coercive Acts descend,
Yet in Philadelphia's hallowed halls, the First Continental Congress convenes,
Washington, Adams, Henry, and Jay, voices of a burgeoning republic,
Denouncing tyranny, proclaiming rights—life, liberty, property.

April's night, shadows deep, Revere's ride through the dark,
The alarm is sounded, Concord's cache must not fall,
Militiamen rise, their resolve firm, the dawn of a new struggle,
In Lexington's fields, Concord's lanes, the first shots fired.

The shot heard round the world—an echo of destiny,
A people awakened, a nation's spirit ignited,
Whitman sings of this birth, this grand emergence,
Of men and women, united in purpose, in liberty's embrace.

I see the lines of battle, the faces stern and resolute,
From farmers' fields, from city streets, a collective voice,
In Whitman's verse, their spirit shines, undimmed by time,
A tribute to the rebel heart, the dawn of freedom's light.

Oh, America, in your youth and vigor, your audacious stand,
In every heart that beats for justice, your spirit lives,
From the Revolution's flames, a nation forged,
In song, your story endures—eternal, vibrant, free.

18

Five Souls for Freedom

Five Souls for Freedom

A veil of shadow cast, an ancient war unfurls,
Beneath the sallow lamp, where history murmurs,
From the abyss of time, the Seven Years' strife,
A conflict vast, seizing new lands under the crown's insidious light.

The coffers drained, the motherland seeks gold,
Imposing taxes, unfurling scrolls,
The Stamp Act, the Townshend burden laid,
A tremor of unrest, the colonies swayed.

The drums of discord beat in distant lands,
In Boston's streets, a cry takes stand,
The air grows taut, a mob, a massacre,
Five souls taken, the powder's bitter stir.

In winter's guise, with feathered guise,
Men of Boston, in twilight rise,
To the harbor's edge, with silent zeal,
The tea descends, in protest's seal.

Imperial wrath, the Intolerable binds,
Coercive chains, where liberty pines,
A congress forms, a voice to reason,
To challenge the crown, in daring treason.

From diverse soils, the delegates convene,
To speak of rights, both heard and seen,
Life, liberty, a trial by jury,
Against the tide of Britain's fury.

Yet conflict brews, a restless tide,
In Concord's field, in Lexington's pride,
A midnight ride, a clarion call,
To arms, to arms, the Redcoats fall.

From this blood, a nation's birth,
In dawn's first light, the cry of earth,
The shot resounds, in history's hall,
The Revolutionary flame, the war for all.

19

A Hymn of Valor, Spilled Blood

A Hymn of Valor, Spilled Blood

On that April night, 'neath a restless sky,
Redcoats march, boots heavy with tyranny's cry,
From Boston to Concord, a purpose grim,
To seize the flames of liberty, to stifle the hymn.

In Lexington's quiet green, a scattered few stand,
Seventy hearts, strong with freedom's demand,
A shot rings out in dawn's early haze,
Who fired first, in the fog of fate's maze?

Eight souls fall, blood mingling with earth,
A costly cry in freedom's birth,
Yet courage blooms where bodies lay,

A spark ignites, a new dawn's day.

To Concord's bridge, where waters flow,
A band of patriots meets the foe,
With hearts unbowed, they face the storm,
Gunfire erupts, the air grows warm.

Two of ours, three of theirs, lives paid in full,
The price of freedom, harsh and cruel,
Yet the Redcoats falter, retreat begun,
A march back to Boston under a rising sun.

Along the road, the patriots chase,
Each step forward, a fierce embrace,
Casualties mount, the struggle clear,
Revolution whispers, freedom near.

Years hence, Emerson's pen would trace,
In lines of honor, the battle's grace,
"By the rude bridge that arched the flood,"
A hymn of valor, of spilled blood.

On July's fourth, the voices rise,
Singing the tale of freedom's prize,
In Concord's fields, where echoes stay,
The shot heard 'round the world that day.

Through words and time, the story soars,
From humble grounds to history's shores,
A testament to the brave who dared,
To stand, to fight, their dream declared.

20

Whispers of Rebellion, Roars of War

Whispers of Rebellion, Roars of War

In the brooding dusk of Philadelphia, they gathered. Faces drawn, lines etched by the weight of time and purpose. A Congress, not of statesmen alone, but of men with a vision to unshackle the chains of an empire. There sat Franklin, wise and wry, and Jefferson, quill poised like a dagger, ready to carve a new destiny from the rough-hewn stone of rebellion.

Spring whispered through the narrow streets, yet the air was thick with the portent of conflict. On Breed's Hill, the first true cry of liberty echoed, a defiant chorus amidst the smoke and blood. Men fell, and in their falling, they stood taller than ever. Bunker Hill became a testament not to a victory lost, but to a spirit unbroken.

Through the long autumn and winter, Washington and his men, ragged yet resolute, held the line. Fort Ticonderoga's cannons rumbled across the frozen ground, and in the chill of March, the British, bloodied and beaten back, retreated to the north. Boston breathed again, free, if only for a moment.

Summer bloomed into fervor. By June, the very air seemed to crackle with the fever of independence. The word itself, independence, held in its syllables the weight of centuries, the promise of tomorrows. The ink was barely dry on Jefferson's parchment when the thunder of British boots signaled a new onslaught.

Howe's fleet, an iron fist in velvet seas, descended upon New York with grim determination. In the stifling heat of August, the Continental Army, outflanked and outmatched, tasted bitter defeat on Long Island's shores. Washington, the stoic general, withdrew, a tactical retreat across the Delaware's cold embrace.

But on Christmas night, with the stars as his silent witnesses, he struck back. Trenton's Hessian guards, drunk on holiday cheer, fell in the surprise of a masterstroke. Princeton followed, a glimmer of hope in the dark days of winter, as the army found its strength once more in the fields of Morristown.

A declaration had been made, and in its making, a nation was born. From the flicker of revolution's flame, a blaze grew. Through the smoke and blood, the cannon's roar and the whispered prayers, they forged ahead, step by faltering step, into the uncertain dawn of independence.

21

Saratoga's Turning Tide

Saratoga's Turning Tide

Once upon a midnight dreary, while the colonies, weak and weary,
Faced the might of British fury, in the year of seventy-seven—
From the north, with doom impending, Burgoyne's army south-
ward wending,
Sought to cleave the rebels' mending, drive them to a shattered
heaven.
Fort Ticonderoga fallen, cast a pall where hope was riven,
Tides of fate were unforgiven.

Burgoyne's march through forests creeping, past the streams and
shadows keeping,
Saw his forces onward sweeping, pressing to the Hudson's shore.
Yet, in southward folly casting, Howe had left his kin unfastening,
Unprotected, Burgoyne, grasping, to the fate he could not floor.

General Gates with rebels grasping, met them at a place of lore,
   Freeman's Farm—blood, battle, gore.

September's chill bore dark intoning, sounds of muskets, cries of moaning,
   As the British found them groaning, 'neath the weight of rebel score.
   Gates, with cunning, all commanding, saw Burgoyne's hopes swiftly sanding,
   On the fields where death was branding, marking each with fearsome lore.
   Freeman's Farm—its tragic standing, first of fates to mete and more,
      Echoes on through history's core.

In October's misty waking, Burgoyne's plight was further aching,
   Bemis Heights bore witness, shaking, with the struggle's final roar.
   Redcoats faltered, spirit breaking, while the rebels, earth's bones quaking,
   Pressed their advantage, forward making, conquest in the theater of war.
   On the seventeenth, forsaking, Burgoyne's troops could fight no more,
      Surrendered, broken, battle-sore.

From this victory, darkly gleaming, flickered hope's frail candle, beaming,
   In the shadows, freedom streaming, heralded by foreign shore.
   France, in secret aid abiding, now in open stance confiding,
   Joined the cause with strength, providing succor in the throes of war.

Thus the conflict, once dividing, Britain and her sons in store,
  Swept the world with furious bore.

Saratoga, turning tide, where the patriots, hearts of pride,
Crushed the might of Empire wide, breaking chains to live
once more.
  Now, forever in the telling, where the winds of fate are swelling,
  Lives the tale of courage, dwelling in the annals, evermore.
  Saratoga, grim, compelling, whispers through the ages' door,
    "Freedom's fight—forevermore."

22

The Birth of an American Ideal

The Birth of an American Ideal

In the verdant twilight of rebellion's dawning hour, a few bold hearts beat with a longing so profound it threatened to fracture the very air they breathed. Amid the strife and early battles, complete severance from the motherland was but a dream held by the radical few, men like John Adams whose vision pierced the veil of tradition and saw the uncharted promise of liberty.

Yet, as the seasons turned and Britain's iron grip tightened, the murmur of independence grew louder. October's chill carried with it the proclamation of King George III, his voice a thunderous decree against the colonies' defiance. The enlargement of the royal forces cast a shadow over the Atlantic, reaching American shores by the new year and igniting a fierce resolve within the hearts of the radicals. The conservatives, once hopeful for reconciliation, found their illusions shattered by the king's unyielding stance.

In January 1776, a pamphlet arrived, stirring the embers of revolution into flame. Thomas Paine, a recent arrival from England, penned "Common Sense," his words a clarion call to the natural rights of man and the imperative of independence. The pamphlet spread through the colonies like wildfire, its influence profound, converting many to the cause of liberty.

Unbeknownst to many, it was Thomas Jefferson who would later craft the defining document of this burgeoning nation. For years, the Declaration of Independence was seen not as the work of a single hand but as a collective cry from the entire Continental Congress.

March brought North Carolina to the forefront, the first to cast its lot with independence, a precedent soon followed by seven other colonies by mid-May. The tide was shifting, the currents of revolution swelling with an unstoppable force.

In the heat of June, Virginia's Richard Henry Lee rose before the Continental Congress, his motion for independence a spark in the tinderbox of debate. The halls of the Pennsylvania State House echoed with impassioned arguments, the air thick with the gravity of the decision at hand. The vote on Lee's resolution was deferred, but the seeds of destiny were sown.

Before their recess, the Congress entrusted a committee of five with a monumental task: to draft a formal statement justifying their severance from Britain. Thomas Jefferson, John Adams, Roger Sherman, Benjamin Franklin, and Robert R. Livingston set quill to parchment, their combined intellect and fervor giving birth to a document that would echo through the ages.

Thus, in the crucible of conflict and the forge of ideals, a new nation began to take shape, its foundation laid not in the blood of battle alone but in the ink of profound vision and unyielding resolve.

23

A Birth Marked by Chains

A Birth Marked by Chains

The hallowed scroll, with ink yet wet,
In Congress wrought, a pledge was set.
"Created equal," the words resound,
Yet silent chains in darkness bound.

A nation's birth, a paradox clear,
Freedom proclaimed, yet shackled by fear.
The cries of those in bondage deep,
In shadowed corners, their secrets keep.

Jefferson's pen, with fire and grace,
Condemned the trade, a human disgrace.
He saw the king's relentless hand,
In distant lands, where horrors spanned.

"He waged cruel war," the draft proclaimed,
"Against human nature," it boldly named.
"Piratic commerce," an "assemblage of woe,"
Yet these truths were struck, their light brought low.

For in the halls where freedom's cry,
Was shaped and formed to reach the sky,
There lay a truth too harsh, too near,
The chains of slaves, the grip of fear.

Southern fields with cotton white,
And northern docks by moonlit night,
All thrived upon this grievous trade,
A dark foundation, deeply laid.

Thus the passage, bold and true,
Was cast aside, its words subdued.
For unity in war's embrace,
Left justice in a shadowed place.

Yet echoes linger, whispers stay,
Of truths obscured in light of day.
A nation born in freedom's name,
Still wrestles with its hidden shame.

The silent clause, a specter's trace,
A legacy, a bitter grace.
For in the quest for liberty,
Lay seeds of future agony.

So as we hail the banner bright,
Let shadows speak of hidden plight.

For every star, each stripe unfurled,
Bears witness to a complex world.

In striving for a brighter morn,
Remember those in darkness born.
Their silenced cries, their unseen tears,
A haunting of our founding years.

24

A Soldier in Silent Valor

A Soldier in Silent Valor

In the hushed, resolute woods of war, there moved
In unseen bravery, the heart of Anne Marie Lane.
With her husband, John, she walked the paths
Where shadows of independence stretched,
And echoes of freedom's cry mingled with the rustle
Of leaves underfoot, a quiet rebellion in stride.

In the garb of a soldier, she carried more
Than musket and knapsack; she bore the weight
Of a nation's nascent hope, wrapped in valor.
No curious eye questioned, no tongue dared to ask—
For in the fury of battle, courage is a garment
Worn by all who dare to fight.

The Battle of Germantown, a cruel testament,

Left her wounded, a silent sufferer,
Her flesh bearing secrets, her resolve unshaken.
She fought, as twilight danced upon the dew,
Until the stars bore witness to her sacrifice,
And her name whispered through the ranks,
A testament to the unseen hands
That shaped the sinews of rebellion.

Mary Ludwig Hays, with pitchers of water,
Quenching the thirst of liberty's soldiers,
Became Sergeant Molly in the cannon's roar.
Her bravery, a fire kindled in the heat of Monmouth,
Recognized by Washington's approving gaze.

Margaret Corbin, with fierce hands,
Manned the cannons where her husband fell,
Her name inscribed with honor,
Her wounds a testament to her sacrifice,
A pension her reward, the first of many
To walk the path where freedom's promise leads.

Yet, beneath the banners and the battle cries,
Women stood, not merely as silent watchers,
But as participants in the great struggle.
Their names, often lost to the silence of time,
Carried the weight of a nation's dreams,
Woven into the fabric of independence.

In the end, Anne Marie Lane, a soldier true,
Retired with her beloved, her body scarred
But spirit unbroken, receiving a pension
In acknowledgment of her extraordinary service.

Her legacy, a silent echo, calls forth
The stories yet untold, the voices yet unheard.

Historians must delve deep into the archives,
Seeking the hidden traces, the whispered tales
Of women who, like Lane, donned the soldier's garb,
And fought with the courage of conviction.
In every faded document, in every forgotten letter,
Lives the testament of those who dared
To carve a path toward liberty.

In the quiet reflections of Richmond,
Where a plaque now stands in honor,
The story of Anne Marie Lane beckons us
To remember, to honor, to seek the truth
Of every soul who fought for freedom's light,
Regardless of the form they wore in battle's night.

25

Hope's Flickering Flame

Hope's Flickering Flame

In the deep and silent winter of Valley Forge, where frost and hardship grip,
Washington's weary soldiers, under skies so cold and gray,
Found in Prussian Steuben's guidance, a discipline they could equip,
And in Lafayette's young valor, a light to guide their fray.
Through the bitter, freezing nights, beneath the stars' array,
    They prepared for dawning day.

On the twenty-eighth of June, with summer's sun to blaze the trail,
Sir Henry Clinton's redcoats moved, their path to New York clear,
From Philadelphia's shadow, where liberty's bell would wail,
Yet Washington's forces rose to strike, Monmouth's fields to sear.

The clash did end in stalemate, yet the patriots held no fear,
    Their resolve did persevere.

July brought forth the Frenchmen, d'Estaing's fleet upon the tide,
With sails aloft and cannons bright, they sought the British main,
A concerted effort rising, with hopes and dreams allied,
But Newport saw ambitions falter, joint endeavors in vain.
Still, the Northern front grew quiet, entrenched in stagnant strain,
    War's rhythm slow and plain.

In those restless, troubled years, the nation's heart did strain and break,
    Arnold's name turned traitor, a dagger to the cause,
    Mutiny's whisper, discontent's murmur, the spirit's strength to quake,
    While in the Southern theater, the British sharpened claws.
    Georgia fell beneath their might, Charleston's siege gave pause,
        Yet hope lived in the laws.

Cornwallis drove his campaign through Carolina's verdant lands,
Crushing Gates at Camden, August's heat a burning brand,
But King's Mountain turned the tide, with patriots taking stands,
October's winds blew victory into the rebel's hand.
Gates displaced by Greene's command, his strategy well planned,
    For freedom they would withstand.

At Cowpens in the dawning year, Tarleton's forces met their match,
    Morgan's men with cunning moved, a victory to claim,
    With valor fierce and tactics clear, they seized the British catch,
    The South's bright star now shining, in liberty's name.

Though battles raged and hopes did clash, the cause remained the same,
    Independence was their aim.

Thus, the war's great tapestry, in North and South alike,
Wove tales of courage, sacrifice, and undying will to fight,
Through winter's chill and summer's blaze, through every battle strike,
The vision of a nation free did guide them through the night.
And in the hearts of those who bled, a future shining bright,
    The dream of freedom's light.

26

A Song of Freedom Rings

A Song of Freedom Rings

In the waning light of 1781, as autumn leaves fell upon the blood-
soaked soil,
General Greene's relentless push, his strategy astute and wise,
Forced Cornwallis and his weary men to Virginia's Yorktown,
toilsome toil,
Where York River meets the Chesapeake, beneath those somber
skies.
French allies joined with Washington, their forces did comprise,
A force to claim the prize.

Rochambeau, steadfast and brave, with Gallic troops in line,
Marched beside the Continental Army, their hearts set on a goal,
With 36 French warships guarding, the British fate entwine,
Cornwallis trapped, his options bleak, his pride to pay the toll.
On October's nineteenth day, defeat did take its toll,

Surrender's bitter roll.

Illness claimed Cornwallis' name, his sword not his to give,
Instead, Charles O'Hara stood, the token to present,
To Rochambeau he offered first, but Washington would live,
By passing to his deputy, the honor thus was lent.
Lincoln took the offered blade, the gesture's full intent,
  The end of war's lament.

Victory at Yorktown's field, though grand, was not complete,
Charleston held by redcoat bands, New York with British might,
For two long years the battle's cry in silence did retreat,
No further blood would stain the earth, no clarion call to fight.
Yet signs of peace began to gleam, an end approached in sight,
  The dawn of freedom's light.

Charleston, Savannah, redcoats gone, the tides began to turn,
In Paris, men with ink and quill did draft the terms of peace,
November saw agreements signed, though fires of war did burn,
September of '83, the treaties brought release.
Britain's crown acknowledged now, American increase,
  Independence, sweet surcease.

Thus closed the chapter, eight years long, of revolution's fight,
From Lexington to Yorktown's yield, a nation forged in strife,
With treaties signed and peace declared, a future shining bright,
The struggle borne on battlefields, gave birth to freedom's life.
In solemn words and courage bold, they ended tyranny's rife,
  A new world free from knife.

So let the annals now record, in Poe's dark, rhythmic prose,
The tale of how a people rose, to claim their liberty,

From shadowed halls of tyrants' rule, to where hope's river flows,
Their story etched in sacrifice, a fight for sovereignty.
In every heart the echo rings, a song of victory,
  Forever bold and free.

27

Washington at Yorktown

Washington at Yorktown

In the October twilight, Cornwallis bowed,
To America's defiant cry, proud.
George Washington, at the summit's peak,
Yet still, for more rungs he seemed to seek.

Years of shadows, betrayal's dark sting,
His spirit wrung by war's cruel, unending ring.
Yorktown's silence, the field's final breath,
Spoke of victory, whispered death.

Yet his heart trembled with each passing day,
Unsure if prideful Britain would stay.
Another year, nerves stretched so thin,
Waiting, watching for the fight to begin.

But the god of war, his hunger sated,
Left Yorktown, a ruin, desecrated.
Virginia's charm, now a reeking waste,
Madness of war's frenzy, bitter taste.

Paris ink dried, redcoats set to leave,
America's dawn, a new reprieve.
November's air, crisp and clear,
Washington's farewell to soldiers dear.

Knox, beloved, led the final march,
Through Harlem's heights, beneath freedom's arch.
Manhattan, barren, homes laid to ruin,
Echoes of fire, memories strewn.

Staten Island's jeers met British disdain,
A cannon's roar, futile and vain.
Washington's men, weary yet proud,
Cheered by patriots, voices loud.

Ill-clad, weathered, yet they stood,
Symbols of a nation, in brotherhood.
Loyalists gone, a new era's dawn,
As dinners and speeches greeted the morn.

December's tavern, a silence fell,
Eight years of war, tales to tell.
Glasses raised, love and gratitude,
Washington's voice, with emotion imbued.

Knox stepped forward, tears in his eyes,
A warrior's embrace, heartfelt goodbyes.

Von Steuben followed, others in line,
Each man's sorrow, a moment divine.

The general's wave, a final glance,
Into the boat, a soldier's trance.
From Jersey's shore to Philly's halls,
To Annapolis, where duty calls.

Commission handed, Knox to lead,
Washington free, from burden freed.
Mount Vernon's hearth, Christmas Eve's light,
A private man, on the silent night.

2 8

The Song of Frank Dalton

The Song of Frank Dalton

I.

I sing of Frank Dalton, the pride of his kin, the beacon of his brothers,

In the year of eighteen eighty-four, commissioned he was, under the iron hand of Judge Parker,

A deputy U.S. marshal, tall and proud, with a heart of steel and a gaze like thunder,

Three years he roamed, through lawless lands, where shadows dance with danger.

II.

O Cherokee Nation, where destiny drew its breath,

On the morning of November twenty-seventh, eighteen eighty-
seven,
    The skies bore witness to a tragedy, a tale of blood and valor,
    The St. Louis Globe Democrat declared to all,
    "A bloody tragedy took place this morning."

III.

    Frank and his men, Bob and Bud Heady, youthful companions
in a world untamed,
    Having delivered the captured to Fort Smith's gates, they rested
by the river's edge,
    In the bottoms, amidst the whispering leaves, with no pressing
call, they tarried,
    Until Jim Cole arrived, with writs in hand, to join their reso-
lute band.

IV.

    Cold was the Sunday, weak the sunlight, as Frank and Cole
warmed by the fire's remains,
    Cole spoke of Dave Smith, a specter in the Indian Territory, a
man marked by the law,
    Two writs against him, for larceny and whiskey's forbidden trade,
    Leaving behind Bob and Bud, the two lawmen set forth, on a
quest of justice's blade.

V.

    Frank, ever the picture of a marshal bold, his attire neat, his
boots polished bright,

A hero from dime novels come to life, tall and lean, unafraid of the night,
With Cole by his side, through autumn's barren arms, they rode,
To a clearing, a camp, a woman by the fire's glow.

VI.

Approaching with caution, their Winchesters drawn, the scene was set,
Cole to the front, Frank to the back, a strategy of practiced might,
The woman cried out, Dave Smith emerged, and with a shot, Frank's chest was struck,
A stagger, a fall, Cole stumbled too, but fate had not yet played its final card.

VII.

Cole's rifle fired, a chaotic ballet of life and death,
Smith thought him dead, but Cole rose and shot true, Smith fell to the earth,
From the cabin, a shot rang out, and Cole, wounded, fled,
A woman's cry, "Lord a mercy, I'm killed!" echoing in the clearing.

VIII.

Behind a tree, Cole sought refuge, exchanging fire with the unseen foe,
Until his ammunition spent, he fled to Fort Smith, a tale of woe,
Miraculously, Frank lived, Dave Smith was slain,
But young Will Towerly emerged, a pistol and Frank's Winchester in hand.

IX.

Frank, pleading for mercy, "For God's sake, don't shoot. I'm already a dead man,"
Towerly, indifferent to the plea, pulled the trigger, sealing Frank's fate,
Satisfied, he rode away, leaving behind the echoes of a hero's end,
Nearby residents approached, the woman dead, her truth told in silence.

X.

Leander Dixon, wounded, and Mrs. Smith, her cries now stilled,
As Emmett Dalton lamented, "Frank is dead. A martyr to his duty,
Reckless days, where good and bad alike fell to the quick shot,
A quivering form, one final twitch, and silence forever."

XI.

From Fort Smith, a posse came, to reclaim the fallen marshal,
Wrapped in blankets, his mangled form, they bore him to Coffeyville,
O Frank Dalton, your name etched in the annals of the West,
A hero, a martyr, in the wild land's relentless quest.

XII.

I sing of Frank Dalton, a symbol of law and bravery,
In the tapestry of time, his story weaves, a thread of honor and strife,

O reader, remember, in the twilight's gentle embrace,
The tale of Frank Dalton, the marshal, the man, the legend of his race.

29

The Underground
Rail-Road

The Underground Rail-Road

A term - coined in jest -
By Thomas Smallwood, who saw,
Through the wide-eyed bafflement of slaveholders,
A secret path for freedom.

In a time of bondage and chains,
Where souls were counted as property,
Smallwood and Torrey,
Heroes of the night, swashbucklers of justice.

With wit and courage,
They carved a path in darkness,
A network of hope and deliverance,

That whispered through the night.

In mocking tones, Smallwood ridiculed,
The baffled enslavers,
Who deemed the enslaved incapable,
Yet watched them vanish, like smoke in the wind.

Oh, the irony they crafted,
A trope of empowerment,
A lash to the oppressors,
The "under ground rail-road" was born.

Boldly they worked,
Not in ones or twos, but by scores,
Whole families, carriage loads,
Liberating the enslaved from the clutches of tyranny.

In their daring deeds,
They hoped to shatter the chains,
Destroy the faith of enslavers,
In the false profit of human misery.

A vision, a strategy,
To make the enslavers see,
That paying for labor,
Was safer, cheaper, more humane.

Smallwood, a figure striking,
Lost to history's shadow,
His deeds, his name,
Deserving of remembrance.

With every risk he took,
For those still in bondage,
He forged a path,
A model for radical action.

In his writings, a voice,
Blunt, shrewd, sardonic,
Ahead of his time,
A satirical masterpiece of truth.

Yet history, in its cruel irony,
Fades his name,
While his bold partner, Torrey,
Is remembered with honor.

In their partnership,
Black and white, hand in hand,
They liberated souls,
From Washington to Baltimore.

Not waiting for the enslaved to flee,
But encouraging, guiding, leading,
They struck blows for liberty,
Against the relentless clock of oppression.

Dangerous enemies they made,
Slaveholders, police, traffickers,
Each escape, a battle,
In a war for human dignity.

The likes of Slatter,
Human trafficker, foe to freedom,

Saw in Smallwood and Torrey,
Lethal enemies to his trade.

Their tales intertwined,
Freedom's light against slavery's shadow,
A terrible, terrifying predicament,
In the mid-Atlantic's borderland.

To flee north, or to endure,
A cruel choice, fraught with peril,
A chapter in the American crime,
That haunts us to this day.

30

Lafayette's Farewell

Lafayette's Farewell

An ancient day, redolent with July's breath—
Lafayette, an ember of a bygone blaze,
Lifts a boy with dawn's innocence,
Kisses a cheek as tender as morning dew.
Brooklyn gathers, hearts swelled with history,
As the old general lays a cornerstone for youth.

Echoes of revolution tremble the air,
The fiftieth year of freedom's birth,
Lafayette, the last luminary of a fading galaxy,
Graces the land, a living relic.
Washington's ghost whispers through time,
Adams and Jefferson, shadows soon to fade,
Their souls destined to depart on liberty's day.

He came from France, a child with riches and dreams,
A nineteen-year-old knight of ideals,
His parents' estates, vast and opulent,
Left him a lord in youth's sweet bloom.
A general, Congress decreed,
A boy who bore the world's weight on slender shoulders.

Wounded in Philadelphia's throes,
He bled for a nation yet unborn.
French lifelines, his gift to a struggling child,
His valor led to Yorktown's fateful end.
Returned to France, to ignite liberty's spark,
His words, a manifesto for humanity's rise,
To the Assembly, he offered hope.

Moderation his mantle, chaos his challenge,
Fleeing Jacobins' ire, confined in Austrian chains.
Years passed in dungeon's dark embrace,
Yet freedom's flame in his heart did blaze.

In August's twilight, his tour began,
Twenty-four states, each one a homecoming,
Washington's crypt, tears etched in marble,
Old soldiers' hands clasped in memory's embrace.
Niagara roared, Erie's waters bore him,
Bunker Hill's stones whispered his name,
Monticello's halls, Jefferson's last embrace.

A kiss bestowed on a boy named Walt,
Future poet, bard of the large-hearted,
He penned of courage, present and past,
Of hearts that embraced a cause beyond self.

Sixty-eight years marked in White House cheer,
Revolution's youth remembered in age,
Risks taken with a young heart's clarity,
Dreams dreamt with a young heart's fervor.
Possibilities seen with eyes unclouded,
Perseverance won the day.

September's dawn, Lafayette's adieu,
A dazzling sun, a crowd in solemn awe,
Adams spoke, tears mingled with words,
"You alone survive," a nation's gratitude.

Twenty-four cannon roared their farewell,
A carriage bore him through silent throngs,
Children perched on shoulders, eyes wide,
Profound silence embraced the river's edge.
History's weight, mortality's whisper,
Heroes' legacies, debts of honor,
All these bound the watchers in reverence.

A launch to the ship, a final wave,
Lafayette, carried home by gentle waves,
A hero's journey, completed, never to return,
Gone, yet forever etched in liberty's heart.

31

A Nation's Promise

A Nation's Promise

March 4, eighteen hundred and one,
A new dawn breaks, Jefferson at helm,
The land of hope and promise,
Bound by rivers, bordered by dreams,
Spanish Florida a southern whisper,
New Orleans, a pulse beneath Spanish sky.

Electoral whispers, Jefferson and Burr,
Thirteen states, a trinity plus three,
Tennessee's hills, Kentucky's wild heart,
Vermont's green cradle of liberty.
Mountains of Appalachia,
A barrier, a bridge, to futures untold.

The land divided—coast and crest,

Tidewater whispers, Chesapeake sighs,
Tobacco's tendrils, slave-laden fields,
FFVs, their legacies entwined.
Jefferson, Madison, shadows of kin,
Land's promise, a haunting refrain.

Hope in rivers, hope in soil,
Hope in freedom's breath.
Inland whispers of coastal disdain,
Rebellion's echo, whiskey's cry,
Shays's ghost in the night,
A nation striving to unify.

Tobacco's yield, a bitter gold,
Virginia's heart, a tale retold,
Planters' hands, slaves' silent screams,
Jefferson's pen, a world unseen.
Freedom's ink, yet chains remain,
Uneasy hearts in liberty's refrain.

A nation's breath, a moral quest,
Slavery's shadow, a haunting guest,
Jefferson's struggle, a torch passed on,
From Washington's gaze to Madison's dawn.
Dreams of wheat, fields of hope,
A vision born, a nation's scope.

New England's shores, winds of change,
Puritan hearts, a righteous range,
Small farms, ships that sailed,
A simpler life, where freedom hailed.
Quakers' call in middle lands,

A softer touch, peace in their hands.

Across the valleys, the Hudson's might,
New York's riches, a glowing light,
Trade and wealth, a complex dance,
Slavery's grip, freedom's chance.
Revolution's flame, questions rise,
Slavery's end, in truth's disguise.

Pennsylvania's cry, abolition's voice,
Franklin's call, a moral choice,
Constitution's pen, a silent plea,
Gradual steps towards liberty.
Jefferson's heart, conflicted beat,
Virginia's path, a slow retreat.

March 4, eighteen hundred and one,
A new dawn breaks, Jefferson at helm,
The land of hope and promise,
Bound by rivers, bordered by dreams,
A nation's journey, a path unseen,
Liberty's quest, a future redeemed.

32

The Wreckage and the Whisper

The Wreckage and the Whisper

Joe Womack waits, a solitary figure
Amid the scholarly crowd, his history
Unearthed from the Alabama Delta,
A relic of the past, the Clotilda's ghost.

In the auditorium, faces attentive,
Expectant eyes fixed upon the stage,
As the tale of the Clotilda unfurls,
A final voyage, a grim testament.

The Deep South's hunger, insatiable,
For bodies to toil in fields of profit,
Defying the edicts, laws of the land,

Timothy Meaher's clandestine plan.

A ship, a hold, human cargo in chains,
Men, women, children—dreams shattered,
The Middle Passage, a corridor of despair,
To the shores of Alabama, their cries unheard.

The war ends, freedom proclaimed,
Yet marooned, these West Africans
Forge a new path, Africatown's birth,
A testament to resilience, to hope reborn.

Womack speaks of their enduring legacy,
The church, the graves, whispers of the past,
Their stories woven into the fabric of his youth,
A legacy he strives to protect, preserve, prolong.

Joycelyn Davis, descendant of survivors,
Speaks of family, tradition, Charlie Lewis,
Echoes of history in the present moment,
Africatown's heart beating through time.

Yet the present shadows the past,
Pollution, industry, a community besieged,
The highways, the factories, a relentless march,
Encroaching on the sacred, the hallowed ground.

Womack, a sentinel, recounts the struggle,
The ash in his drink, the lost friends,
A lifetime of witnessing, bearing the weight,
Of a history both harsh and profound.

He speaks of monuments, not in stone,
But in lives lived, in memories held,
In the community's essence, a testament
To survival, to the human spirit's strength.

The Clotilda's wreckage, now revealed,
A stark reminder of the past's hold,
Yet also a beacon, a call to remember,
To honor those who endured, who lived, who fought.

In the quiet of the auditorium,
Womack's words resonate, a plea, a promise,
To safeguard Africatown's future,
To let its story be told, heard, and felt.

For though the same forces linger,
The legacy of those brought over,
Their strength, their spirit,
Remains unbroken, unyielding.

The wreckage of the Clotilda lies beneath,
But its story, its people, rise above,
A chapter of history, a legacy of resilience,
A future shaped by remembrance, by hope.

33

Ballad of Annie Oakley

Ballad of Annie Oakley

In the heart of Darke County, where the wild winds blow,
A girl named Phoebe Moses would soon let her prowess show.
Born on August thirteenth, in eighteen-sixty's dawn,
Her father's old Kentucky rifle she would soon don.

Her father, Jacob Moses, felled by pneumonia's grasp,
Left behind six hungry mouths, and a widow's quiet gasp.
Annie, at just six years old, saw two fathers taken by fate,
Yet through the trials and hardships, she would not break nor wait.

To the Darke County Infirmary, young Annie went to stay,
Learning skills of sewing and care, she made her own way.
By fourteen, she returned, a hunter, keen and bright,
With a rifle and a steady aim, she put small game to flight.

In Greenville's shops, her quarry sold, to Cincinnati it flew,
Till word spread far and wide of what young Annie could do.
Jack Frost, a hotelier, called her to a challenge fair,
Against Frank E. Butler, a sharpshooter with skill rare.

At fifteen, she bested him, twenty-five shots out of twenty-five,
Frank missed just one, but in that match, a love would soon revive.
Annie's aim entranced him, and soon they were wed,
On August twenty-third, their lifelong path was led.

Together they traveled, their showmanship a draw,
With dog George in their act, they filled crowds with awe.
In St. Paul, she met Sitting Bull, who gave her the name
"Little Sure Shot," for her precision and modest fame.

Joined with Buffalo Bill, the Wild West show,
Annie's star ascended, her name began to grow.
In England's Queen Victoria's Jubilee, she shone,
Her shooting skills unrivaled, she stood alone.

Across Europe they traveled, a seasoned star so bright,
Shooting ashes off cigars, her talent pure delight.
Women found in her a model, Buffalo Bill declared,
That shooting was for all, a healthy exercise to be shared.

In nineteen-o-one, a train crash caused her pain,
Yet she continued performing, with Butler she remained.
They retired in Cambridge, a quieter life to seek,
But the lure of the arena soon made their future bleak.

When war came in seventeen, she offered once more,
To lead a regiment of women, to fight on foreign shore.
Rejected once again, she trained soldiers in her way,
Giving time to the Red Cross, her dog Dave led the fray.

Years passed, and retirement called, but boredom soon set in,
Annie sought a comeback, her passion a burning within.
In twenty-two, an accident took her back a step,
Yet she rose again to perform, with strength and pep.

In twenty-six, her health declined, back to Ohio she went,
With Frank beside her, through fifty years they were spent.
She penned her memoirs, their love story pure,
Annie Oakley passed, and Frank followed her cure.

In fields of Darke County, where the wild winds blow,
The legend of Annie Oakley continues to grow.
A sharpshooter, a performer, a loving wife,
Her story an epitome of courage and life.

34

Wild Bill Hickok and the Ballad of the Diamond

Wild Bill Hickok and the Ballad of the Diamond

In Kansas City's streets, where shadows dance and play,
Walked Wild Bill Hickok, who bathed every day.
A gunslinger so famed, with sharp eyes keen and bright,
He graced the gaming tables, dressed in fine attire, light.

He led missions with the Army, a guide so bold and true,
From trail to saloon, his legend only grew.
But there was another field where his spirit found delight,
The corner of Fourteenth and Oak, where the Antelopes took flight.

A young sport called baseball, its diamond rough and raw,
Captured Bill's keen interest, held his heart in awe.

He watched the Antelopes, beneath the sun's hot blaze,
And played with local children in the Kansas City haze.

One Saturday, a challenge came, to umpire the great game,
For brawls had marred the matches, and tempers were aflame.
The Antelopes faced Pomeroys, the crowd was tense with fight,
But Hickok, with his Colt six-shooters, would keep the peace the
that night.

The game commenced with fervor, the crowd held bated breath,
Yet each call by Hickok dispelled the threat of death.
He stood behind the plate, with authority and grace,
His presence stilled the chaos, his gaze set the pace.

No fist or boot or bottle, no knife could find its mark,
With Hickok as the umpire, there was no chance for dark.
The Antelopes won proudly, forty-eight to twenty-eight,
The crowd roared their approval, for Wild Bill's umpired fate.

He bowed to their applause, a smile upon his face,
Then to Market Square he wandered, to resume his gambling
pace.
A life so filled with daring, with cards and guns and fame,
Yet baseball's simple pleasure, a spark within his flame.

Years later in Deadwood, his vision dimmed with time,
He sought to win his fortune, in a land far less sublime.
A tragic end awaited, in a saloon's darkened door,
Shot from behind, the legend fell, to rise again no more.

Yet on that dusty diamond, where the Antelopes once played,
Hickok's spirit lingers, in the summer's light arrayed.

A gunslinger, an umpire, a man of many roles,
His story weaves through history, as timeless as the coals.

For in the heart of Kansas, where the wild winds blow,
Lies the tale of Wild Bill Hickok, and the game he came to know.
In Yeatsian verse, we honor him, a figure brave and grand,
Who tamed the wild with wisdom, and held the diamond's hand.

35

The Song of Custer

The Song of Custer

In New Rumley's humble soil, where winters bite and chill,
A child was born, a restless boy with an iron will.
George Armstrong Custer, your name a whisper in the breeze,
A spirit of the frontier, where the wild heart never flees.

In Michigan's green embrace, you found a fleeting home,
With half-sister's hearth and husband's strength, you were free to roam.
Schools of the North shaped your days, your future yet unspun,
Teaching gave you bread and warmth, but adventure drew you on.

West Point's stony halls called you forth, a cradle of command,
Yet discipline's chains could not bind the dreaming in your hand.
Demerits piled like autumn leaves, your spirit soared aloft,

The "goat" they named you, last in line, but your heart was ever soft.

The drums of war echoed loud, the nation split asunder,
You stood amidst the thunderclaps, where brave souls tore asunder.
From Bull Run's first chaotic roar to Gettysburg's bloody plight,
You rode with valor, brash and bold, a warrior in the night.

Libbie's love a beacon bright, in war's relentless fray,
Her letters carried whispers sweet, on each long, blood-soaked day.
Together you faced the world's wild edge, through trials thick and thin,
A bond of hearts, a meld of souls, where battles cease to spin.

In Appomattox's quiet dawn, where Lee's proud flag did fall,
You stood a hero in the sun, heeding honor's call.
Sheridan's gift, a table's grace, for deeds both great and small,
Libbie's hands held history's weight, in memory's eternal thrall.

Westward then, the journey led, to plains of endless sky,
Where Sioux and Cheyenne roamed the earth, with spirits soaring high.
The Washita's cold river ran with tales of victory told,
Yet shadows grew, resentment brewed, within the ranks, it smoldered cold.

At Little Bighorn's fateful banks, your final stand was made,
A clash of wills, a surge of fate, beneath the sun's fierce blade.
Divided forces, scattered cries, the dust of battle rose,
And in that storm, your luck ran dry, amidst a thousand woes.

Naked beneath the vast blue sky, unscalped, but death's cold mark,
A bullet to your fearless heart, a darkness swift and stark.
Your name became a legend's thread, in history's vast loom,
A martyr to some, a villain to others, your tale etched in the gloom.

Libbie's pen kept flames alight, in widow's endless night,
Her words a bridge to times now past, where memory burns bright.
Through books and tales, your spirit soared, above the mortal fray,
A figure grand, a hero damned, in history's sweeping play.

George Armstrong Custer, your song is bittersweet,
A melody of courage bold, and of defeat's retreat.
In the echoes of the ages, your name shall ever ring,
A testament to glory's call, and the sorrow it can bring.

36

Ode to Simon Kenton

Ode to Simon Kenton

In the cradle of Virginia, where Fauquier's fields lie wide,
A boy was born to farm and toil, with simple dreams inside.
Simon Kenton, frontiersman, your legend deeply sown,
From youthful scuffles to boundless wilds, your daring spirit shown.

At sixteen years, in passion's heat, you fled your home in haste,
Believing blood was on your hands, you left no time to waste.
As Simon Butler, you took flight, to Ohio's rugged breast,
Where rivers whispered tales untold, and fate's hand gave you rest.

Two years you hunted, woods your home, a scout with vision keen,
Lord Dunmore's War, you played your part, in shadows evergreen.

To Boonesborough, Kentucky's heart, you brought your fear-
less soul,
  Where Boone's brave fort stood sentinel, against the British roll.

  April dawned with danger near, the Shawnee at the gate,
  But in that hour, your courage clear, would alter history's fate.
  Boone's scouts you joined, to warn, defend, to stand against
the tide,
  With musket's roar and fervent heart, your valor far and wide.

  In cornfields' green and battle's gray, the Shawnee warriors
sprang,
  With rifles raised and tomahawks, the air with fury rang.
  Yet you, Kenton, swift and sure, with eye and aim so true,
  Saved Boone from death's impending clasp, through fields of
morning dew.

  As bullets flew and men did fall, you bore the wounded chief,
  With strength of limb and will of iron, you gave the fort relief.
  Jemima joined your desperate flight, her father in your arms,
  Boonesborough's walls welcomed you, and sheltered from alarms.

  Through gauntlet's cruel, unyielding trials, the Shawnee tested
might,
  You stood as stone, endured their wrath, and earned their grim
respect.
  Cut-ta-ho-tha, the condemned, yet in their tribe you found,
  A place, a name, a strength renewed, on sacred, ancient ground.

  With Clark you marched, Fort Sackville's prize, the Revolution's
thread,
  Northwest conflicts, battles fierce, where many warriors bled.

Mad Anthony's call you heeded true, the Mad River Valley's claim,
A scout, a leader, soldier strong, with courage as your flame.

Two loves you knew, in life's embrace, with children round you grew,
Through fire's loss and tender bonds, your heart found strength anew.
Brigadier General, Ohio's pride, in War of 1812's harsh fray,
At Thames you saw Tecumseh fall, and spared his form's decay.

Simon Kenton, legend grand, your life a tale so vast,
A beacon in the wilderness, a hero from the past.
Through trials, wars, and love's embrace, your spirit ever bright,
In Ohio's fields, your legacy, a testament to light.

Now rest, brave soul, in Urbana's earth, where history softly sings,
Your story etched in nature's heart, and borne on eagle's wings.
A frontiersman, a savior bold, your name forever free,
Simon Kenton, hero true, in the land of liberty.

37

Ode to Cousins, Boone and Morgan

Ode to Cousins, Boone and Morgan

In days of yore, when forests vast spread wide,
Two kindred souls from Wales did fate betide.
Daniel Boone, a tracker keen, of Blue Ridge fame,
And Daniel Morgan, ruddy faced, from Shenandoah came.

Their blood entwined, yet paths apart they walked,
Until Braddock's ill-fated march they stalked.
In Cumberland's fort, 'neath banners bright they stood,
Boone with his waggon, Morgan, strong of wood.

The British marched with colors high, through timber dense,
Ignoring wisdom from the men, whose senses were immense.
Boone in the rear, sharp-eyed, his instincts keen,

Morgan, towering, drove his team, a daunting scene.

Through Monongahela's ford, they trudged with might,
Unaware of shadows poised to strike in twilight.
The forest thick, the path a winding trap,
The French and Shawnee ready for the snap.

The musket's crack, the arrows' deadly flight,
Braddock's men fell swiftly in the fight.
Boone and Morgan, sensing doom, prepared,
For the ambush sprung, the British unprepared.

Boone, with deftness, cut his horse and rode,
Into the wilds, where safety might abode.
Morgan, struck by ball through cheek and neck,
Refused to fall, his spirit none could check.

They rallied forth, amid the chaos dire,
Through musket smoke and woods afire.
The retreat was fierce, the Redcoats fled in fear,
While Boone and Morgan fought, their courage clear.

From Braddock's folly, they emerged anew,
Heroes unsung, yet hearts so true.
Morgan healed, his legend yet to grow,
In Revolution's tide, his might would show.

At Cowpens field, his strategy so grand,
With riflemen and militia he took his stand.
Tarleton's forces fell in dire dismay,
Morgan's brilliance won the day.

Virginia's gift, a land of vast expanse,
His life a testament to fate's romance.
Boone, the trailblazer, bound for western skies,
In wilderness and freedom, his spirit lies.

Cousins born of Welsh descent, their paths did cross,
In moments fraught with danger and with loss.
Yet from those woods where echoes still remain,
The tales of Boone and Morgan we retain.

Oh, frontier sons, your legacy so bright,
In tales of old, your valor lights the night.
From Braddock's march to Cowpens' bloody field,
Your names endure, your legends never yield.

In life's great tapestry, your threads are gold,
Brave Boone, bold Morgan, stories told.
Two kindred spirits, bound by blood and strife,
Forever etched in history's vibrant life.

38

The Darkened Heart of
Pierce

The Darkened Heart of Pierce

Beneath the pale New Hampshire sky, where shadows linger, low,
A man of sorrow, Franklin Pierce, did rise amidst the snow.
In youthful years, he took the helm, the nation's yoke to bear,
Yet fate did weave a mournful tale, a tapestry of despair.

A marriage made in trembling hands, with Jane, a somber bride,
Her frail form, both heart and mind, in ceaseless torment tied.
She loathed the halls of power's play, where her husband's path was laid,
And in her grief, she saw the curse, by which their lives were swayed.

Three sons they bore, yet two were claimed by death's relent-
less hand,
    And Jane, she wept, in fervent prayer, for God's inscrutable plan.
    In time, a third, young Benny, bright, became their beacon light,
    But shadows crept and sorrow's grip turned day to endless night.

    In Andover, the wheels of fate did spin with ghastly force,
    A broken rail, a shattered dream, a child's lifeless course.
    The cap he wore, now bloodied, torn, beneath the timbered
wreck,
    And Jane awoke to horrors vile, her mind a shattered speck.

    In Washington, the oath was sworn with hands upon the law,
    For Pierce, his heart a hollow void, in public's gaze did thaw.
    No grand parade, no festal cheer, no partner by his side,
    A nation's helm, a grievous weight, where piercing sorrows bide.

    Within the White House, shadows loomed, a spectral First Lady,
    In rooms she roamed, with letters penned to sons in purgatory.
    Her fragile mind, a haunted vale, where whispers echoed clear,
    And Pierce, he turned to spirits strong, to drown his every tear.

    The bottle's edge, his solace sought, in amber's liquid glow,
    Yet leadership eluded him, as tides of darkness grow.
    A troubled time, a fractured land, with Kansas bathed in strife,
    And Pierce, he stumbled, lost in woe, amidst his tragic life.

    No second term, no laurels won, his legacy lay bare,
    A tragic figure, broken down, in history's cruel snare.
    For in the end, the shadows won, and madness claimed its prize,
    A presidency marred by grief, beneath the nation's skies.

Yet in those days of haunted halls, where shadows intertwined,
The tale of Pierce and Jane reveals the fragile human mind.
For in their sorrow, one can see the echoes of a plight,
Where love and loss, in tragic dance, are lost to endless night.

39

Lincoln's Legacy in Words of Grace

Lincoln's Legacy in Words of Grace

In days of strife and darkened skies, where justice found no place,
There stood a man with thoughtful eyes, and words of measured grace.
From humble start to halls of power, his voice did rise and swell,
To speak of unity and hope, where fractured nations dwell.

In Lyceum's ancient echoes, first his diagnosis came,
Of passions wild, and laws defied, and demagogues of fame.
He warned of perils deep within, of liberty's disdain,
And urged a fervent faith in law, to heal a nation's pain.

Then Gettysburg, where fields of red bore witness to the cost,
Of freedoms won and freedoms lost, in battle's bitter frost.

With brevity, his words did soar, above the bloodied plain,
A dedication to the cause, that none had died in vain.

Yet in his second inaugural, the height of his ascent,
Where every phrase was forged in fire, and each word's weight
was bent.
He spoke of war's divine decree, a penance to be paid,
For sins of "American Slavery," in truth and light displayed.

No "southern" crime, no "African" chain, but nation's shared
disgrace,
A sin that bound both North and South, in guilt's embracing
trace.
With wisdom, he invoked the past, two centuries of toil,
To show the threads of history, in blood and human soil.

His voice transcended vengeful calls, he sought a higher aim,
To guide a torn and weary land, through charity's warm flame.
"One eighth," he said, "of all our kin, were colored, bound, and
chained,
Not scattered, but confined below, where liberty was feigned."

He saw them not as numbers cold, nor just a southern blight,
But part of Union's living soul, deserving equal right.
In "Southern part" he chose his words, to bind the fractured
whole,
A single nation, unified, with liberty its goal.

In closing lines, he called for peace, a lasting, just embrace,
Where malice waned and charity, could heal a nation's face.
His speeches, though succinct and brief, bore wisdom's timeless
gleam,

A beacon for the years ahead, a nation's hopeful dream.

So let us heed the lessons taught, in Lincoln's hallowed speech,
To find in words and deeds alike, the unity we seek.
For in his eloquence we see, a path through darkest night,
A journey toward a fairer world, where justice shines its light.

40

The Ambush

The Ambush

James Boone lay bleeding, beneath the shadowed crest,
Where frozen earth and fate had brought his final rest.
A plea to end his suffering, met with stoic gaze,
From Big Jim, once a friend, now lost in war's cruel maze.

The dawn had barely whispered, when raiders struck the camp,
Their war cries split the morning, their knives and axes damp.
The Mendinall boys were first, their laughter turned to cries,
While Crabtree fled to forest depths, beneath the sullen skies.

An older slave fell quickly, a tomahawk's grim kiss,
Another found a hiding place, in timber's dark abyss.
Young Drake, though mortally wounded, sought refuge in the wild,
His body found months later, cold rock his grave defiled.

James Boone, with gutshot wound, could barely grasp his knife,
Beside him Henry Russell, cut down from future life.
Their cries for mercy silenced, beneath the brutal hand,
As Big Jim watched with hardened eyes, a soul made out of sand.

October's chill was settling, as Boone's heart beat its last,
While up the road his father, prepared to move, steadfast.
But James's party's silence, stretched long into the day,
And Daniel Boone grew anxious, as twilight slipped away.

The plan had been so simple, to carve a path anew,
For families seeking fertile lands, beneath the sky's bright blue.
They camped near Cumberland's gateway, with hope in every
heart,
Unknowing that the fates conspired, to tear their dreams apart.

Captain Russell found the scene, a sight of ghastly war,
His son's corpse marred by arrows, James Boone in blood and
gore.
The stolen cattle wandered, the flour and salt were gone,
But Henry's Bible, wrapped in oil, lay untouched, forlorn.

With shovels, picks, and sorrow, they dug the frozen earth,
Squire Boone with burial cloths, from James's mother's hearth.
They wrapped the dead in woolen shrouds, a journey's end
too soon,
The slain were laid to rest beneath October's waning moon.

The painted hatchets circled, a declaration clear,
That war was now upon them, and death was ever near.
Squire Boone spoke of defense, of barricades to build,

For none could tell the number of those the darkness filled.

In history's vast ledger, the clash would not relent,
As tides of white and native blood, into the soil were spent.
Yet in this place of mourning, where dreams and lives were lost,
The cost of seeking frontier's edge was paid in bitter frost.

The vision of a land so free, unburdened by the past,
Met with the harsh reality, that shadows ever cast.
For every step of progress, for every mile won,
Came with the price of innocence, and blood beneath the sun.

4I

The Balance of Power

The Balance of Power

Three branches intertwine, a woven braid,
Of power, deftly balanced, never swayed.
The executive, a potent, guiding hand,
Commands the nation, laws at its demand.

Yet checks arise, from halls where laws are born,
In Congress, voices loud and varied, sworn.
To craft the rules that bind us, keep us free,
A thousand voices singing harmony.

But should one branch, with ambition, swell,
The framers knew this tale, this urge too well.
So Congress, bold, with veto power, stands,
The President's decrees within its hands.

And if the President should turn away,
From bills presented, chosen to delay,
Congress, steadfast, can override the slight,
Two-thirds must join, in unity and might.

And still, the robe of justice, black and grand,
Watches over all, with gavel in hand.
The Supreme Court, guardians of the law,
Reviews the statutes, finding every flaw.

With Marbury and Madison, they claimed,
The right to strike down laws that are inflamed.
Unconstitutional, they deem with care,
Ensuring justice, balanced, true, and fair.

Impeachment looms, a specter in the night,
For those who stray from duty, wrong for right.
Congress wields this power, grave and strong,
To judge the President when acts go wrong.

The purse strings too, they hold with tight control,
To temper whims of power, checks patrol.
And term limits, a guard against the reign,
Of power unchecked, in humble bounds remain.

Yet, when the branches clash, as oft they do,
Supreme Court stands, with wisdom, guiding through.
Executive commands can be reversed,
By judges who ensure our laws are versed.

In balance, power thrives, a dance of old,
With checks and balances, our tale is told.

Ambition counteracts ambition's fire,
And keeps our fragile freedom, ever higher.

In this great system, intricate, profound,
Where human flaws in wisdom's web are bound,
The framers' vision, in the Constitution sealed,
A nation's strength in balanced power revealed.

42

An Ode to Equality

An Ode to Equality

In a land where dreams were cast in ink,
Upon a parchment bold,
The words declared in fervent hope,
A story to be told.

Helen Hamilton Gardener stood,
Against the tides of scorn,
With science as her steadfast sword,
A new dawn to be born.

"Examine this," she dared to say,
"Of brain and gender, find,"
Yet truth revealed—no difference vast,
But sameness of the mind.

Through decades, science whispered clear,
In DNA's embrace,
That 99.9%,
No race, nor creed, nor face.

Yet here we stand, in shadow's grip,
The dream still seeks the light,
For inequality persists,
A constant, weary fight.

The rhetoric of freedom's song,
Sings sweet in pledged refrain,
Yet actions speak, and louder still,
Of justice we must gain.

From Birmingham to Watts' red flames,
The echoes of the past,
Remind us of the road we trod,
The freedoms we amassed.

A mother's fight for credit earned,
A sister's talents spurned,
Injustice cloaked in daily norms,
And love in shadows turned.

Equality, a lofty dream,
In Jefferson's own hand,
"Life, liberty, pursuit of joy,"
A right for every man.

Yet whispers rise, a forceful "no,"
From those who fear to share,

Their privilege clutched in tightened fists,
Blind to what's fair.

But listen close, a growing hum,
A chorus in the street,
From Black Lives Matter's fervent cry,
To every voice we meet.

The rhetoric of lofty words,
Is not enough, we know,
For real equality demands,
In actions it must show.

Equality is more than phrase,
More than a hollow sound,
It's in the steps we take each day,
To lift from off the ground.

For ideas, as Victor Hugo said,
Invade with mighty force,
Yet need the will, the mind's own fire,
To set a true course.

In 1776, a dream,
In words both bold and bright,
Yet here, today, that dream remains,
A beacon in the night.

Equality, a forceful hope,
Not mere abstraction's claim,
But in the hearts of every soul,
It lights a fervent flame.

We battle still, for truth, for right,
For freedom's full embrace,
To honor all, in every life,
In every creed and race.

So rise, and act, let actions speak,
Of justice and of peace,
For in our hands, the power lies,
To make the struggle cease.

From Helen's stand to present day,
Our journey has begun,
To see each soul, in equal light,
Until the battle's won.

43

Washington's Orchard Dream

Washington's Orchard Dream

In August's humid, heavy air,
Retired from battle's scarred domain,
Strode Washington, with brow of care,
In fields where dreams and duty strain.

The laurels of his war-earned fame,
He set aside for soil and seed,
Yet thoughts of freedom's fragile flame,
And nation's needs, within him breed.

Monetary woes, defenses weak,
These shadows dark his restful days,
Yet sweeter visions oft would sneak,

In orchard's sunlit, verdant maze.

Barbados once, in youth he roamed,
Where citrus trees their treasures bore,
Oranges, lemons, flavors honed,
And pineapples he did adore.

"None pleases my taste as do's the pine,"
He wrote with fervor, young and keen,
In Mount Vernon, he'd design,
A grove where tropic fruits were seen.

But winters harsh in Virgin's land,
Could wither dreams of citrus gold,
So Washington, with patient hand,
Sought knowledge from the ancients old.

Greenhouses of the Romans' past,
Where emperors their greens would save,
And Europe's lords in wealth amassed,
With glass and warmth, their gardens brave.

Yet in this new, republic's soil,
Such grand constructs were yet so rare,
But Washington would not recoil,
For Baltimore's green Mount Clare.

The Carrolls, bold in faith and deed,
Had built a house for plants to thrive,
Despite the prejudice they'd heed,
Their lush domain kept hope alive.

To Maryland, his gaze he turned,
To learn the secrets glass could yield,
And in his heart, a fire burned,
For citrus groves in fertile field.

From enemy to friend alike,
He gathered wisdom, seed, and skill,
For freedom's cause, he took the hike,
And for his orchard, bent his will.

So Washington, with dreams entwined,
Of nation strong and garden bright,
Saw both in citrus groves aligned,
A future blooming, fair and right.

In August's haze, his mind would trace,
From wars of past to peaceful soil,
Where fruits of labor, time, and grace,
Would bloom in freedom's fertile toil.

44

A Meditation on the
Electoral College

A Meditation on the Electoral College

In the shadows of our Constitution's birth,
Where framers' visions mingled with the earth,
An institution stands, misunderstood,
Its essence lost in time's relentless flood.

The College of Electors, ancient scheme,
By many seen as but an idle dream,
When popular vote yields not the victor's crown,
A deeper disquiet in our hearts is found.

Five times, the tally split from common voice,
And left the nation grappling with its choice.
Undemocratic, some decry its form,

A relic of an age, a privileged norm.

Yet deeper still, within those hallowed halls,
The founders' wisdom etched upon the walls,
Debates on federalism's fragile thread,
To balance power, thus our nation's spread.

Madison, with pen and paper poised,
Sketched out a plan, his intellect employed.
For Wilson sought a vote by people's hand,
While Sherman feared the rise of tyrant's stand.

So here we stand, in modern discontent,
With calls to end what many now resent,
Yet in the core of federal design,
The College holds a purpose, clear and fine.

Not slavery's tool, as some have claimed,
But a device for balance it was framed.
Each state, a voice, a sovereign in its right,
To cast its vote within the federal light.

Lincoln's victory, a testament so clear,
By College won, though popular vote was near.
Without this structure, might we now reflect,
The march of history we'd not expect.

And yet the doubts, they linger in the air,
Is this device still just, still truly fair?
In layers of electors, some see flaws,
An echo of democracy's lost cause.

The states, they predate union's tight embrace,
Their voice preserved in this contested space.
Without the College, federalism fades,
And with it, states' distinct and cherished shades.

Efficiency was not the founders' goal,
But liberty, a precious, fragile soul.
The College stands, a guard against the tide,
Of fleeting passions, undemocratic ride.

So as we ponder changes in our sphere,
Let's weigh the costs, the truths that must be clear.
For in this age-old system, flawed though seen,
Lies the essence of a union's dream.

Abolish not with haste, but with deep care,
For federal design is delicate and rare.
The Electoral College, misunderstood,
Yet in its core, a legacy of good.

45

At City Tavern, 1777

At City Tavern, 1777

At City Tavern, by the flicker of the flame,
Washington and Lafayette, two names in history's frame,
August's breath upon them, they planned and they schemed,
Along the Delaware's banks where freedom's light beamed.

Philadelphia trembled, braced for the fray,
Fortifications stood tall, defenses in array.
Invited to the tour, Lafayette would soon see,
The fledgling army's strength, their fight to be free.

Come August's eighth noon, beneath Germantown skies,
The marquis gazed upon soldiers with discerning eyes.
Eleven thousand strong, yet poorly armed they stood,
Clad in hunter's shirts, jackets of rough-hewn wood.

No uniforms bright, no banners unfurled,
Just men of the land, fighting for a new world.
The generals assembled, Stirling, Greene, Knox, and Stephen,
Men of mixed fortunes, by conviction driven.

Stirling, brave yet lacking in judicious stride,
And Stephen, often found in an intoxicated tide.
Washington watched, his heart heavy with the sight,
Of a ragtag force ready to fight for the right.

"We should be embarrassed," Washington sighed,
"To show ourselves to one of French pride."
But Lafayette, with wisdom beyond his years,
Said, "I am here to learn, not to bring fears."

Humility spoke, in tones soft and sincere,
A European's grace, rare to hear.
Among the ranks, his words took root,
A young marquis with valor, earning repute.

To Little Neshaminy Creek, they then did move,
A stone house, Moland, their strategy to prove.
In modest manners, Lafayette did dwell,
With Washington's family, his story to tell.

Timothy Pickering noted, with a thoughtful gaze,
The marquis had joined, in those early days.
A young man from France, of lineage grand,
Now stood with the rebels, to fight for the land.

In unity they forged, under peril and strife,
Dreams of liberty, a nation's new life.

At City Tavern, and fields beyond,
Washington and Lafayette, in history, fond.

46

The Unanimous Declaration

The Unanimous Declaration

When in the course of human tides,
A people rise, with hope as guides,
To cast off chains of tyrant's grip,
And set their sails on freedom's ship.

In Congress, on July Fourth's gleam,
A dream was born, a nation's dream.
Thirteen states, united, free,
Declared their right to liberty.

"We hold these truths," their voices rang,
"All men created equal," sang.
Endowed by God's own hand with rights,
Life, liberty, and joy's sweet flights.

Governments, from consent, arise,
Yet, when they fail, it's no surprise,
That people choose to break away,
To seek a brighter, freer day.

A history of grievances told,
Of kings and laws both harsh and cold.
Refusal to assent, neglect,
Oppression's rule, a dark effect.

He called assemblies far and wide,
To wear them down, to break their pride.
He shut down houses, blocked their vote,
And crushed their rights with every note.

Obstructed justice, laws denied,
With judges bound to kingly pride.
New offices to harass and drain,
A standing army's bitter reign.

Taxes imposed without consent,
Their trade cut off, their pleas unspent.
For every wrong, a tyrant's hand,
For every hope, a stifled land.

Yet still they sought in humble plea,
Redress of wrongs, their aim to be.
But tyranny's ear was deaf and cold,
A prince unfit, a tale retold.

Thus, to the world, they now proclaim,
A right to life, a nation's name.

Free and independent states,
With power to choose their own fates.

In solemn pledge, with sacred vow,
Their fortunes, lives, to God they bow.
In freedom's light, a nation born,
A hope that shines through darkest morn.

O let this tale of courage stand,
A testament, a guiding hand.
For in the course of human strife,
The quest for freedom, the breath of life.

47

Echoes in Holmes County

Echoes in Holmes County

In the whispers of Holmes County,
Where horse-drawn buggies glide
And bank barns touch the sky,
The past and present merge,
An echo of simpler times.

Fields tilled by hand,
By the strength of beasts,
Not machines, but spirit,
A faith that moves the plow,
That shapes the land with patience.

Men with beards, hats wide-brimmed,
Women in modest gowns,
Organdy caps that hold

The prayers of centuries,
Softly whispered in the dawn.

Yet, beyond the bucolic charm,
A history etched in pain,
Of Anabaptists fleeing,
Of lives lived in secret,
Of faith forged in fire.

Michael Sattler, a monk transformed,
His words, the Schleitheim creed,
Written with conviction,
Sealed with martyr's blood,
A testament to belief's endurance.

Dirk Willems, a tale of grace,
Escaping icy fate,
Returning to save his captor,
A selfless act,
A life extinguished, yet enduring.

From Swiss hills to Pennsylvania's plains,
The Amish journeyed, seeking peace,
In William Penn's promise,
A land where faith could breathe,
Where hands could work in freedom.

Holmes County, a second home,
A sanctuary of toil and tranquility,
Where each sunrise
Is a nod to those before,
Who lived, who died, for simple truths.

No longer hunted,
Their gatherings open,
A testament to resilience,
To a way of life
That bends but does not break.

In fields and farms, their legacy,
In prayers and hymns, their hope,
A community bound by love,
By the quiet strength
Of faith unyielding.

So when you see their buggies pass,
In the gentle Ohio breeze,
Remember their journey,
Their enduring light,
And smile, for in their peace, we find our own.

48

Sons of Liberty

Sons of Liberty

In the darkened streets where shadows weave,
Where moonlight doth the cobbles cleave,
A whisper stirs, a breath so bold,
Of liberty, its tale retold.

From taverns dim and alley's end,
A brotherhood begins to mend,
The chains that bind, the shackles tight,
They vow to break in darkest night.

Their spirits high, their courage true,
A flame that through the twilight grew,
With ink and quill, with sword and pen,
They pledged their lives, these noble men.

The whispers grew to fervent cries,
Beneath the ever-watchful skies,
For freedom's cause, they stood as one,
Until the final fight was won.

Oh, Sons of Liberty, revered,
Your name through ages ne'er feared,
For in your hearts, the fire burned,
And through your deeds, our freedom earned.

In sepulchres where heroes sleep,
Their secrets in the silence keep,
We honor you, our guiding star,
Who showed the way through war's cruel scar.

So let us raise our voices high,
And to the heavens send our cry,
For Sons of Liberty, we stand,
Defenders of our precious land.

49

Daughters of Liberty

Daughters of Liberty

In shadows deep where moonlight gleams,
Beyond the realm of waking dreams,
The Daughters rise, with hearts afire,
Their courage pure, their cause entire.

Within the quiet, secret rooms,
Where hope dispels the darkest glooms,
They gather close, their voices hushed,
Yet in their hearts, rebellion rushed.

With threads of silk and flaxen weave,
They spun their dreams, they dared believe,
In liberty, in freedom's song,
For which they'd strive, endure the long.

Their hands, so skilled, their minds so bright,
Did fashion tools for freedom's fight,
Not with the blade, but with the craft,
They wove a tale of justice's raft.

Each whisper shared, each glance exchanged,
Within their eyes, the fire ranged,
For tyranny they would defy,
Beneath the wide and watchful sky.

Oh, Daughters brave, your tale is told,
In every thread, in every fold,
Your strength, a beacon in the night,
Guides us toward the path of right.

In echoes soft of yesteryears,
Your legacy, it still appears,
A testament to courage true,
The light of freedom shone through you.

So let us sing your praises loud,
For in your deeds, we stand unbowed,
Daughters of Liberty, so dear,
Your spirit lives, we hold you near.

50

Committees of Correspondence

Committees of Correspondence

In dusky rooms where candles flicker low,
Where shadows dance and secret whispers flow,
A covenant of minds begins to form,
A beacon 'midst the brewing storm.

From colony to colony they write,
With quills dipped deep in freedom's light,
Dispatches swift through night and day,
In clandestine, courageous array.

Upon the parchment, thoughts take flight,
Defiance penned in ink so bright,
Each missive, bold, a cry for right,

A spark against the tyrant's might.

Through courier's hands, the messages passed,
In fervent haste, through shadows cast,
A network strong, a lifeline true,
Uniting hearts of varied hue.

These scribes of justice, fierce and keen,
In corridors where none are seen,
Did weave a web of bold discourse,
A silent yet relentless force.

Oh, Committees, vigilant and wise,
With fire within your steadfast eyes,
You crafted paths for freedom's call,
And stood as one against the thrall.

In every letter, hope was sown,
In every word, a seed was grown,
For liberty, you paved the way,
And lit the dawn of a brighter day.

So let us hail your noble cause,
Your secret works that gave us pause,
Committees of Correspondence, grand,
Your legacy shall ever stand.

51

Continental Congress

Continental Congress

In halls where echoes softly tread,
Beneath the beams where visions spread,
The Continental Congress met,
With hearts aflame, their purpose set.

In earnest tones and fervent plea,
They spoke of rights and liberty,
From every corner, voices rose,
Against the crown, their stance they chose.

Each delegate, with valor bright,
Did stand as one in freedom's light,
In ink they scribed, in voice declared,
Their dreams, their hopes, their justice bared.

With wisdom keen and tempers bold,
They shaped a future, strong and gold,
The parchments filled with fervent script,
The dawn of freedom firmly gripped.

From dawn to dusk, through night's embrace,
They forged a path for freedom's race,
Debates did roar, decisions weighed,
A nation's course in words was laid.

Oh, Continental Congress, brave,
In you, the seeds of hope did crave,
A fertile ground where dreams could grow,
Against the tide of tyrant's woe.

Your legacy, in history's tome,
A beacon bright, a guiding home,
For in your halls, the nation's birth,
Did echo forth to span the earth.

So let us honor, let us raise,
A song of thanks, a voice of praise,
Continental Congress, wise,
Your spirit in our hearts does rise.

52

Minutemen

Minutemen

Along the whispering edge of dawn,
Where shadows linger, thin and drawn,
The Minutemen with steadfast stride,
A silent, waiting countryside.

Time measured not in hours' grace,
But in the pulse of urgent chase,
Each tick a beat, each moment spun,
As daylight breaks, their watch begun.

Among the whispers of the trees,
A murmur soft on every breeze,
They stand alert, in twilight's fold,
A prophecy of courage told.

Their eyes, the stars, their breath, the wind,
Their hearts, in unity, unpinned,
From hearth and home, from fields so green,
They rise, unseen, in times serene.

At sudden cry, at distant drum,
The call to arms, their blood becomes,
With muskets raised and purpose clear,
They vanish into morning's veer.

Oh, Minutemen, in shadows cast,
Your legacy through time will last,
In every echo, every field,
Your valor's tale, forever sealed.

The morning sun, the evening's fall,
Your silent steps, we still recall,
For in the dawn's relentless hue,
The Minutemen stand brave and true.

Their lives a whisper in the dawn,
Yet in their hearts, a strength is drawn,
For freedom's call, they wait and then,
Like shadows, fade to earth again.

53

Continental Army

Continental Army

In fields where dawn meets dusk's embrace,
Where dreams of freedom interlace,
The Continental Army stands,
With grit and hope, in rugged bands.

From every hearth and distant shore,
They gather 'neath the flag once more,
With weathered hands and steadfast eyes,
Resolved to claim their destined prize.

Through bitter cold and summer's blaze,
They march in unison, always,
The drumbeat of a nation's heart,
In every stride, they play their part.

In tattered coats and worn-out shoes,
Through battles fierce, their strength renews,
With Washington to lead the way,
They fight for dawn's enduring ray.

From Bunker Hill to Valley Forge,
In every camp, they forge and forge,
A legacy of courage bright,
Against the storm, they hold the light.

Oh, Continental Army, brave,
Through trials deep, you dared to pave,
A path for freedom, broad and wide,
With honor, as your constant guide.

Each scar and wound, each silent tear,
A testament to what is dear,
For in your sacrifice, we see,
The price of cherished liberty.

So let us raise our voices high,
And to the heavens lift our cry,
Continental Army, strong,
In you, our hopes and dreams belong.

54

George Washington

George Washington

O captain of our nascent dreams, whose steady hand,
Did steer the ship of freedom to its destined land,
Upon the fields of valor, where the winds did blow,
Your spirit soared, unyielding, in the ebb and flow.

With eyes that gleamed with wisdom deep, a beacon bright,
You stood, unwavering, through the darkest night,
Beneath the stars, with heavens wide, you made your stand,
The father of our liberty, across this land.

In battle's roar, in winter's bite, through trials stern,
Your courage burned, a steadfast flame, we still discern,
With every step, with every word, you carved a way,
For generations yet to come, for a brighter day.

O Washington, in marble halls, your echo rings,
Through ages vast, your legacy forever sings,
A tale of honor, strength, and grace, a guiding star,
For we, the people, hold you near, no matter how far.

Upon the Potomac's gentle flow, your spirit drifts,
In every breeze, in every dawn, your presence lifts,
The hearts of those who seek the path of justice true,
Inspired by the noble deeds that lived in you.

So let us sing, with voices loud, in praise and cheer,
For George, our guide, our sentinel, forever dear,
In every heart, in every land, your name shall bloom,
A symbol of our freedom, dispelling gloom.

55

Marquis de Lafayette

Marquis de Lafayette

Amidst the velvet shadows of the night,
Where moonbeams dance with whispers soft and light,
A noble figure from a distant shore,
Lafayette, whose heart for freedom bore.

From gilded halls of France's grand chateau,
To battlefields where liberty did glow,
Your spirit soared on wings of fervent fire,
With valor pure and dreams that did aspire.

Oh, Lafayette, through tempest and through storm,
Your courage shone in every steadfast form,
A chevalier of justice, brave and true,
With freedom's light, you pierced the morning dew.

In twilight's hush, where echoes softly play,
Your name, a melody, in hearts will stay,
A hero's song, entwined with honor's thread,
In every land where liberty is spread.

O Lafayette, your spirit grand and bright,
Bridged oceans vast beneath the starlit night,
In revolution's waltz, so fierce and fair,
You danced with destiny, beyond compare.

So let us raise a toast with vintage fine,
To Lafayette, whose heart with ours align,
In every breath, in every whispered prayer,
Your legacy, a perfume in the air.

For in your deeds, the fleur-de-lis does bloom,
In fields where freedom casts away the gloom,
Marquis de Lafayette, revered, adored,
Your spirit graces our eternal shore.

56

John Adams

John Adams

Amid the fervent dawn of liberty's birth,
Where ideals sparked and vision found its worth,
John Adams stood, a statesman bold and bright,
With fervor keen, he fought for what was right.

From Braintree's fields to halls of grandeur vast,
His voice resounded, echoing through the past,
With intellect and passion intertwined,
He shaped a nation, steadfast and aligned.

In congress halls where freedom's light did gleam,
His words like flint, igniting every dream,
A patriot's heart, unyielding in its cause,
He penned the truths that formed our sacred laws.

Beside his peers, in struggle and debate,
He forged the bonds that time would not abate,
With Abigail, his partner, wise and true,
Together, they the seeds of justice threw.

Through storms of war and trials of the heart,
His spirit never wavered, nor did part,
From Paris' courts to London's distant shore,
He championed freedom, opening every door.

Oh, John, whose fervent soul did never rest,
You gave this land your utmost, and your best,
A legacy of service, bold and grand,
A guiding light upon our cherished land.

In every school, in every court and home,
Your wisdom's echoed, evermore to roam,
For in the fabric of our nation's core,
Your name shall ring, remembered evermore.

So let us honor, with our voices clear,
John Adams, patriot, forever dear,
In every heart, in every righteous deed,
Your spirit lives, our country's noble creed.

57

Benjamin Franklin

Benjamin Franklin

In the heart of the city, where wisdom flows,
Amid the hum of commerce, where the river slows,
There stood a man of wit and wide acclaim,
Benjamin Franklin, an enduring name.

With curious mind and boundless, questing zeal,
He harnessed lightning, made the heavens reel,
Through storms of thought and innovation's spark,
He lit the way, a beacon in the dark.

From printing press to halls of stately grace,
His presence felt in every cherished place,
With quill in hand, and spectacles askew,
He penned the words that freedom's breath imbue.

Inventor, statesman, philosopher so wise,
He gazed with insight into distant skies,
From almanacs to treaties, broad and far,
He wove a legacy, a guiding star.

In tavern meetings and salons' bright gleam,
He stirred the hearts, inspired the dream,
Of unity, of justice, grand and pure,
A nation's soul, in liberty secure.

Oh, Franklin, sage of old and new,
Your vision vast, your purpose true,
You bridged the gap 'tween age and youth,
With humor, wit, and timeless truth.

From bifocals to kites that danced in storm,
Your intellect took every form,
In every bolt of lightning's flare,
Your spirit soared, untamed, aware.

So let us raise a glass in homage due,
To Benjamin, our mentor, through and through,
In every book, in every striving mind,
Your essence lingers, ever intertwined.

For in the annals of our cherished land,
Your name is etched by freedom's hand,
A testament to all that we can be,
Inspired by your boundless ingenuity.

58

Thomas Jefferson

Thomas Jefferson

Amidst Virginia's verdant fields so wide,
Where freedom's seed in fertile soil did bide,
Thomas Jefferson, with pen in hand so deft,
Crafted the words that left a nation's breath.

In Monticello's shade, where dreams did soar,
He penned the Declaration's timeless lore,
With eloquence that stirred the hearts of men,
He voiced the truths that rang from glen to glen.

A scholar's mind, with ideals pure and bright,
He sought to guide with wisdom's gentle light,
From natural rights to governance anew,
He shaped a vision, clear and ever true.

In Paris' halls, where diplomats did meet,
He brokered deals with grace and keen deceit,
A statesman bold, in diplomacy's art,
He played his role with intellect and heart.

Yet, flaws and contradictions did he bear,
A man of principles, yet slaveholder's snare,
His legacy, a tapestry so vast,
Reflects the struggle of a nation cast.

Oh, Jefferson, amidst the moral storm,
Your vision shaped our nation, bold and warm,
From Jeffersonian ideals' golden gleam,
To struggles faced, and dreams yet to redeem.

In every word, in every marble hall,
Your spirit lingers, heeding freedom's call,
For in your dreams, in liberty's refrain,
We find our hopes, our promise to attain.

59

Samuel Adams

Samuel Adams

In Boston's streets, where whispers sparked a flame,
A voice arose, igniting freedom's name,
Samuel Adams, fervent and profound,
A patriot's heart in liberty unbound.

With quill and tongue, he stirred the restless throng,
In taverns' warmth, where passions deep and strong,
Did brew the thoughts of revolution's call,
Against the yoke of tyranny's enthrall.

His words, like fire, spread through cobbled lanes,
A clarion call that broke the oppressor's chains,
From Sons of Liberty to battles' roar,
He rallied souls for freedom evermore.

In meetings held beneath the lantern's glow,
With fervent speech, he struck the final blow,
Against the crown's unjust and cruel decree,
He championed the cause of liberty.

From Boston Tea Party's defiant stand,
To every fight that swept across the land,
Samuel, with resolute and steady hand,
Did guide the cause with courage grand.

Oh, Adams, fierce, your spirit's flame,
In every heart that seeks the same,
A testament to justice, pure and bright,
A beacon in the darkest night.

Your legacy, in freedom's breath,
In every land, in every depth,
Shall echo through the ages vast,
A symbol of our freedom cast.

So let us raise a cheer so loud,
For Samuel Adams, strong and proud,
In every word, in every deed,
Your spirit lives, our hearts you lead.

60

Patrick Henry

Patrick Henry

In quiet halls where shadows softly creep,
A voice arose from silence deep,
Patrick Henry, with fervent heart,
Spoke words that tore the night apart.

Amidst the murmur of the crowd,
With gentle strength, so fierce and loud,
He cried for liberty's sweet breath,
A vow that whispered life from death.

"Give me liberty," his ardent plea,
"Or give me death," his soul set free,
A clarion call, so pure, so clear,
That even silence seemed to hear.

In gentle light of candle's glow,
Where words like autumn leaves did flow,
He stirred the embers of the soul,
With passion's fire, he made them whole.

Oh, Patrick, in the twilight's grace,
Your spirit haunts this sacred place,
Where dreams of freedom gently lie,
Beneath the vast, unyielding sky.

In every heart that longs to be,
In every mind that dares to see,
Your legacy, a whisper still,
Of courage wrought by iron will.

So let us honor, soft and true,
The man who brought the dawn's first hue,
With words that pierced the silent night,
And brought the darkened world to light.

61

George Mason

George Mason

In shadows where the cypress trees entwine,
And whispers of the past in silence pine,
George Mason, with a quiet strength did rise,
A champion of the people's rights, so wise.

In Gunston Hall, where thoughtful musings lay,
He penned the words that would not fade away,
The Bill of Rights, a testament so grand,
With quill in hand, he forged a freer land.

A gentle soul with purpose pure and bright,
He stood against oppression's darkest night,
With reasoned voice, he crafted every line,
Ensuring liberty's enduring shine.

In every clause, a spark of justice gleamed,
In every word, a nation's promise dreamed,
For rights inherent, sacred, and bestowed,
He shaped the path where freedom's river flowed.

Oh, Mason, in your tranquil, steadfast way,
You gave the future light of brighter day,
A legacy of fairness, deep and true,
Within our hearts, your spirit echoes through.

In every law, in every right we claim,
Your voice, a whisper, always calls our name,
For in your vision, clear and justly drawn,
We find the dawn of freedoms brightly spawned.

So let us honor, in the quiet morn,
The man whose thoughts of liberty were born,
George Mason, guide and guardian dear,
Your legacy we hold forever near.

62

Crown Officials

Crown Officials

In twilight's deep and shadowed gloom,
Where whispers creep from silent tomb,
The Crown's officials, grim and stern,
In halls of power, did discern.

Beneath the flag of red and gold,
With hearts by royal edicts told,
They served the crown, unwavering, true,
Through every dawn and midnight blue.

The governors in mansions grand,
With justice clenched in iron hand,
The judges robed in solemn might,
Did pass decrees in velvet night.

Their oaths to king and country sworn,
In loyalty, their hearts were torn,
For in the land of rising strife,
They walked the edge of double life.

Through whispers in the shadowed court,
Where secrets dark and truths distort,
They held the line, they kept the law,
Amidst the colonists' rising awe.

Oh, Crown's officials, in your stance,
You danced a grim, precarious dance,
Between the crown's demanding call,
And whispers of rebellion's thrall.

In marble halls where silence dwells,
In echoes of the ancient bells,
Your legacy, in shadows cast,
A story of the loyal past.

So let us whisper soft your name,
In reverence of your steadfast claim,
For in the annals of this land,
Your tale of loyalty will stand.

63

Anglicans

Anglicans

In hallowed halls where candles flicker dim,
Where hymns arise in sacred, solemn hymn,
The Anglicans, in faith's embrace,
Did find their place, their loyal grace.

Beneath the arches, stone and old,
Where stories of the past are told,
Their hearts to England's church were tied,
In reverence, they did abide.

With prayers whispered soft and low,
And echoes of the organ's flow,
They knelt in pews, in shadows cast,
In devotion to the crown steadfast.

In stained glass light, where saints did glow,
They felt the pull of lands they know,
Across the sea, in mother's arms,
Away from rising rebel alarms.

Their loyalty to crown and creed,
A steadfast bond in time of need,
For in their faith, they found the way,
To honor king and church, to pray.

Oh, Anglicans, with hearts so pure,
In trials deep, you did endure,
The whispers of rebellion's cry,
Yet to your faith, you did not fly.

In chapels where the light did bend,
You found your solace, found a friend,
In faith and crown, you stood as one,
Until the rising strife was done.

So let us speak with voices clear,
Of Anglicans who held so dear,
Their faith, their loyalty, their name,
In history's book, forever the same.

64

Merchants

Merchants

In bustling ports where ships did sway,
And golden coins by lantern's ray,
The merchants thrived, with goods so grand,
Their loyalty to Britain's land.

In markets where the voices blend,
And fortunes rise and swiftly bend,
They found their place, their wealth secure,
In trade with Britain, bond so pure.

With spices, silks, and teas in store,
With barrels brimming, ever more,
They saw in crown and trade their path,
Away from revolution's wrath.

Their ships did sail on seas so wide,
With British flags above the tide,
In commerce' heart, they placed their trust,
And viewed rebellion's cause as dust.

For in the gold and silver bright,
They found their reason, found their light,
To stand with crown, to keep the peace,
And let their trading never cease.

Oh, merchants of the bustling quay,
In shadows of the revolution's spree,
You held your ground, in profit's name,
While others fought for freedom's flame.

In every ledger, every trade,
Your loyalty to Britain laid,
A testament to fortunes made,
In history's shadowed promenade.

So let us speak of merchants' tale,
Who rode the tides with every sail,
Their story etched in trade's grand lore,
In history's book, forevermore.

65

Thomas Hutchinson

Thomas Hutchinson

In Boston's streets where murmurs grew,
And shadows in the twilight flew,
There stood a man of steadfast grace,
With loyalty etched upon his face.

Thomas Hutchinson, the governor stern,
In halls of power, did discern,
The rising tide of discontent,
The fervor of rebellion's scent.

With regal bearing, calm and wise,
He met the colonists' fierce eyes,
Their cries for freedom, wild and free,
Against the crown's authority.

In chambers where the ink was wet,
With decrees that the crown had set,
He held his ground, through fire and strife,
Amidst the storm of freedom's life.

The Boston Tea Party's midnight raid,
In shadows deep, the plans were laid,
And Hutchinson, with troubled mind,
Saw loyalty and freedom blind.

His mansion burned, his name reviled,
In times so dark, so fierce and wild,
Yet through it all, he stood his ground,
In loyalty to the crown, profound.

Oh, Thomas, in the tempest's roar,
Your tale is writ forevermore,
In history's pages, dark and bright,
A figure in the loyal night.

So let us whisper, soft and low,
Of Hutchinson, who faced the woe,
A governor in troubled time,
His loyalty, a solemn chime.

66

William Tryon

William Tryon

In New York's halls where shadows fall,
And echoes haunt the council's call,
William Tryon, with steady hand,
Governed the land as crown's command.

From royal seat to city street,
His presence strong, his purpose neat,
He upheld laws with firm resolve,
In loyal service, did evolve.

Amidst the bustling urban sprawl,
Where merchants thrived and traders tall,
He steered the course of governance,
With loyalty, a stalwart stance.

Through tumult's rise and patriot's cry,
He stood beneath the azure sky,
A figure of authority,
In times of colonial liberty.

His mansion grand, his office high,
Bore witness to the rebel's cry,
Yet Tryon held his loyalty,
In service to the crown so free.

Oh, William, in the city's fold,
Your loyalty in tales retold,
A governor with steadfast might,
In history's ever-turning light.

So let us speak, in reverent breath,
Of Tryon's rule, through life and death,
A loyal figure, brave and true,
In history's tale, forever due.

67

Joseph Galloway

Joseph Galloway

In Philadelphia's halls of old,
Where tales of freedom's saga told,
Joseph Galloway, with measured voice,
Argued for peace, a reasoned choice.

A delegate to Congress fair,
With wisdom deep and earnest care,
He spoke for unity and grace,
In hopes to find a middle place.

Amidst the fervor and the storm,
Where passion's fire did transform,
He sought a path of compromise,
To mend the rifts, to heal the cries.

His voice, a plea for calm and peace,
In echoes soft, the tensions cease,
For reconciliation's hand,
To bridge the gap, to heal the land.

Yet in the end, the die was cast,
And independence won at last,
Galloway's hopes, a distant dream,
In history's course, a quiet stream.

Oh, Joseph, in your quest so brave,
To find a way to heal and save,
A nation torn by strife and woe,
Your efforts in the past do glow.

In every debate, in every plea,
For unity and harmony,
Your legacy, in history's scroll,
A tale of peace, a patriot's goal.

So let us honor, soft and low,
The man who dared to seek the flow,
Of compromise and common ground,
In freedom's land, where hope is found.

68

Guy Carleton

Guy Carleton

Amid the rugged wilds where rivers flow,
And whispers of the forest softly grow,
Guy Carleton, with steadfast gaze so keen,
Led British forces 'cross the land serene.

From Quebec's walls to distant shores,
He marched with honor, battles roared,
A general with strategic mind,
In wilderness where fate aligned.

Through valleys deep and mountain's height,
He commanded armies, strong and bright,
With courage forged in fire's glare,
He faced the rebels' bold declare.

In every fort, in every hold,
His soldiers brave, their hearts so bold,
They stood against the patriot's might,
In loyal service, through the fight.

Oh, Carleton, with honor true,
You led your troops, a valiant crew,
Through snow-capped peaks and leafy glen,
Defending crown, defending men.

In history's annals, your name is found,
A leader firm, with vision sound,
In every battle, every fray,
Your loyalty did light the way.

So let us raise a cheer so high,
For Carleton, beneath the sky,
A general of steadfast might,
In Britain's cause, a shining light.

69

Native Americans

Native Americans

Beneath the vast and open sky,
Where ancient spirits whisper nigh,
The Native tribes, in silence strong,
Were caught amid the conflict's song.

From forests deep to plains so wide,
They watched the settlers' growing stride,
Some chose to stand with British hand,
While others sought the colonists' land.

In every heart, a sacred tie,
To earth, to sky, to eagle's cry,
Yet torn between the warring call,
They faced the storm, stood brave and tall.

With wisdom old and stories deep,
They sought a path where peace could creep,
But treaties made were oft betrayed,
Their lands, their homes, in shadows laid.

Oh, Native tribes, in shadows cast,
Your struggle through the ages passed,
In unity and fractured plight,
You sought to keep your people's light.

In every battle's fiery dance,
In every broken treaty's lance,
Your spirit rose, resilient, true,
Amidst the red, the white, the blue.

So let us honor, soft and clear,
The tribes who faced the storm so near,
Their voices echo, strong and free,
In every wind, in every tree.

For in their hearts, the land's embrace,
They held the hope of future grace,
A nation's story, intertwined,
With Native spirits, strong and kind.

70

French Allies

French Allies

Across the ocean's deep expanse,
Where waves caress with gentle dance,
The French, with hearts of solidarity,
Embraced the colonists in clarity.

With ships that sailed on freedom's tide,
And banners raised, side by side,
They lent their aid, both bold and true,
To fight oppression, break through.

In battles fierce, on fields so red,
They stood with courage, never fled,
From Yorktown's plains to Saratoga's blaze,
They turned the tide in war's harsh maze.

With Lafayette and Rochambeau,
Their names in history's ledger glow,
Their arms and gold, their steadfast might,
Brought liberty's triumphant light.

Oh, French allies, in friendship's grace,
You found in colonists a kindred face,
In unity, you fought the fight,
To forge a future, clear and bright.

In every cannon's thunderous roar,
In every victory, evermore,
Your legacy, a bond so deep,
In freedom's land, forever keep.

So let us raise a toast so grand,
To French allies across the land,
In history's tapestry, you shine,
A beacon bright, a steadfast sign.

71

New England Tavern: Paine and Sam Adams

New England Tavern: Paine and Sam Adams

In the dim-lit haven, amidst the scent of oak and ale,
Two kindred spirits meet, their purpose clear as day,
Thomas Paine, with quill in hand, a firebrand of liberty,
And Samuel Adams, sage of the streets, the voice of the throng.

"Ah, Brother Paine," quoth Adams, his eyes aflame with fervor,
"Your words, a clarion call, rouse the soul from slumber deep,
'Common Sense,' they name it, yet uncommon its power,
To stir the hearts of men, to break the chains of kings."

Paine, with earnest gaze, leaned closer to the flame,
"Brother Adams, it is the breath of freedom I seek,
A world where man stands tall, no tyrant's yoke to bear,

In this tavern, let us forge the dreams of liberty."

The tavern's hum recedes, as these titans of the cause,
Exchange the sacred whispers, of a nation yet conceived,
"Freedom," Adams murmurs, "is the seed we plant tonight,
In the fertile soil of minds, where rebellion finds its might."

"Aye," Paine concurs, his voice a river's roar,
"Revolution, it is the cry that echoes in the streets,
From the cobbled alleys of Boston to the fields of Lexington,
The spirit of the free, it shall not be quenched."

Around them, patriots gather, drawn by the flame of discourse,
The air electric, crackling with the promise of a new dawn,
In this humble tavern, where ale and dreams are poured,
The birth of a nation, in whispered words, is sworn.

"Liberty or death," Adams declares, his fist upon the table,
"We shall not bow to tyranny, nor to the crown's cruel hand,
With quill and sword, with heart and voice, we stand,
In defiance, in unity, for the freedom of this land."

Paine, with a nod, lifts his tankard high,
"To the revolution, to the cause we hold so dear,
Let the tyrants tremble, let the oppressed arise,
In this tavern, we forge the fate of the brave and the free."

The fire flickers, casting shadows long,
As Paine and Adams, visionaries bold,
Speak the words that shape the future, in a New England night,
Their spirits intertwined, in the cause of right.

Thus, in the humble tavern's glow, the future's seed is sown,
By Paine and Adams, men of vision, men of stone,
Their conversation, a beacon, in the fog of tyranny,
A testament to liberty, for all posterity.

72

Ben and William Franklin in a Tavern

Ben and William Franklin in a Tavern

In a tavern's warm and shadowed glow,
Where candles flicker, soft and low,
Ben Franklin sat with thoughtful grace,
His son beside him, face to face.

"Dear William," Ben's voice rich and wise,
"Our land's in flames, 'neath freedom's skies.
The cause is just, the path is clear,
Yet I see conflict, pain, and fear."

"Father," William spoke, his tone sincere,
"Your vision's bright, but doubts appear.
The crown, our past, our honored name,

I see the colonies as wild, untamed."

"The colonies," Ben's eyes did gleam,
"Are birthed from hope, from freedom's dream.
Our rights, our voice, they seek to bind,
But liberty is the light we find."

"Yet Father," William's brow did crease,
"Can war and strife bring lasting peace?
The crown's our lineage, duty-bound,
In loyalty, our roots are found."

Ben leaned in, his gaze so keen,
"Change is painful, paths unseen.
But future's bright for those who dare,
To break the chains, to breathe free air."

A silence fell, the tavern's hum,
A quiet space where thoughts did come.
William sighed, his heart at war,
Between the past and future's door.

"Father," he spoke, with voice subdued,
"Our paths diverge, yet both pursued.
May history judge our deeds with grace,
And peace find us in its embrace."

They raised their cups, a silent toast,
To futures forged, to pasts like ghosts.
In that warm tavern's shadowed light,
Two Franklins shared the revolution's night.

73

John Adams and Captain Preston in a Tavern

John Adams and Captain Preston in a Tavern

In a dimly lit tavern, shadows play,
John Adams and Captain Preston lay,
Their thoughts amidst the ale and smoke,
On revolution's brink they spoke.

"Captain," John's voice, a steady stream,
"The conflict's harsh, like a fevered dream.
Yet justice calls, in every breath,
To navigate 'tween life and death."

Preston leaned in, his eyes a storm,
"Adams, I've seen the streets transform.
The cries of 'massacre' still ring,

My men and I caught in the sting."

"Yes," John replied, with lawyer's grace,
"I defended you, in that fierce case.
For law and order must prevail,
In liberty's pursuit, we sail."

"But Adams," said the Captain, low,
"In Boston's streets, the tensions grow.
The crown's grip tight, the rebels bold,
The future's path, in conflict's hold."

"The path is fraught," John's tone was grave,
"Yet to the cause, our hearts we gave.
To build a nation, strong and free,
From tyranny's yoke, we must flee."

Preston sighed, with memories dark,
"Your vision clear, yet leaves its mark.
In service to the crown, I stood,
Now torn between, misunderstood."

"Captain," John said, his gaze sincere,
"The fight for freedom, fierce and near,
Demands we question, stand, and see,
The cost of chains, the price of free."

Their cups they raised, a silent pact,
In tavern's glow, where shadows act.
Two men, from sides opposed, now find,
In shared respect, their paths aligned.

74

Benedict Arnold and General William Howe in a Tavern

Benedict Arnold and General William Howe in a Tavern

In a tavern dim, with lanterns low,
Benedict Arnold and Howe's eyes glow,
Their voices hushed, the ale's embrace,
In shadows deep, they find their place.

"Arnold," said Howe, with soldier's pride,
"The tides of war are fierce and wide.
Your choice to turn, a daring feat,
In conflict's grip, where futures meet."

"General," Arnold spoke, eyes intense,

"My path is paved with consequence.
A patriot's heart, now torn in two,
Between the cause and loyalty due."

"Your valor, known on fields of red,
In Saratoga where you led,
Now turned to king, a fateful stride,
In revolution's restless tide."

"Howe," Arnold sighed, his gaze astray,
"The rebels' cause, I did betray.
But in their ranks, corruption's hand,
Led me to seek a different land."

"Yet in this tavern, shadows cast,
We speak of future, not the past.
Your name now rings in loyal halls,
As freedom's rise, with conflict calls."

"General," Arnold's voice was firm,
"To crown's embrace, I did affirm.
But in my heart, a battle rages,
Between two worlds, in history's pages."

"Arnold," said Howe, with quiet might,
"In war, we choose, we face the night.
Your journey's tale, both dark and bright,
Will echo through the endless fight."

They raised their cups, in solemn cheer,
Two figures bound by fate so near.
In tavern's glow, their stories blend,

In war and loyalty, they find an end.

75

❦

Martha and Abigail in a Tavern

Martha and Abigail in a Tavern

In a quiet corner, softly lit,
Where candles flicker, shadows flit,
Martha Washington and Abigail,
In whispered tones, their thoughts unveil.

"Dear Martha," Abigail began,
"Our husbands lead this noble plan.
In fields of war and halls of state,
They shape the future, seal our fate."

"Mistress Adams," Martha's voice was calm,
"Our roles, though different, bring a balm.
To hearts that break, to homes we tend,

We serve this cause, as steadfast friends."

"In letters long, my thoughts I share,
With John, in hopes to ease his care.
For in his mind, the future's clear,
Yet doubts and fears are ever near."

"Martha, your George, a leader strong,
In him, the hopes of many throng.
You stand by him, through thick and thin,
Your strength, a light in war's dark din."

"Abigail, your wisdom's known,
In every word, your courage shown.
While men may lead with sword and pen,
Our influence flows through them."

"True," Abigail sighed, her gaze afar,
"We guide their hearts, their guiding star.
In every battle, every strife,
We hold the fabric of their life."

"Together," Martha softly spoke,
"We weave the threads that cannot break.
In tavern's quiet, here we stand,
Two women strong, hand in hand."

They raised their cups, a gentle cheer,
In unity, they cast their fear.
In tavern's glow, their spirits blend,
In friendship deep, until the end.

76

Minute Men and Redcoats in a Tavern

Minute Men and Redcoats in a Tavern

In a tavern filled with quiet cheer,
Ten Minute Men and Redcoats near,
Their eyes alight with cautious gaze,
In firelight's soft, dancing haze.

Minute Men:

One stepped forward, voice sincere,
"Our cause for freedom, strong and clear.
In Concord's fields and Lexington,
We fight until our work is done."

His comrade nodded, firm and proud,

"In liberty, we shout aloud.
With muskets ready, hearts afire,
We strive for what our hopes require."

Another spoke, with steady hand,
"For justice, for our native land,
We stand against the crown's command,
In unity, our steadfast band."

Redcoats:

A Redcoat rose, with voice controlled,
"Our duty to the crown, we hold.
From England's shores, we crossed the sea,
To quell rebellion's fierce decree."

His fellow soldier, calm and true,
"In red we fight, the loyal few.
For king and country, we obey,
Through battles grim, both night and day."

Another added, with quiet might,
"Our mission clear, to set things right.
With discipline and order strong,
We stand where we have stood so long."

Together:

In tavern's warmth, the two sides met,
Their eyes a mix of pride and regret.
A Minute Man, with thoughtful tone,
"We fight for home, for land we own."

A Redcoat nodded, slow and sure,
"Our cause is just, our duty pure.
Yet here we stand, in tavern's light,
Two sides of one great, bloody fight."

They raised their cups, a solemn cheer,
For futures bright, for homes held dear.
In tavern's glow, their spirits blend,
Two foes by fate, yet men, and friends.

77

Paine and Hutchinson in a Tavern

Paine and Hutchinson in a Tavern

In a tavern filled with tense, dark air,
Thomas Paine and Hutchinson glare,
Their words like swords, sharp and bright,
In shadows deep, they spark the fight.

Thomas Paine:

"Pompous Hutchinson," Paine began,
"Your loyalty is to a tyrant's hand.
You preach of order, crown, and state,
Yet bind us all to a traitor's fate."

"Common Sense" in Paine's fierce tone,

"For freedom's cause, we stand alone.
No king, no crown, should rule our land,
It's time to break from Britain's hand."

Thomas Hutchinson:

Hutchinson's eyes, with fire burned,
"Rebel Paine, you've much to learn.
Order's kept by crown's firm grip,
Not by your wild, misguided lip."

"Chaos reigns where rebels tread,
Destruction follows where you've led.
In loyalty, our peace is found,
Not in your cries, loud and unbound."

Thomas Paine:

"Peace?" Paine sneered, his voice a lash,
"In chains and fear, your words are trash.
True peace lies in freedom's call,
Not in the crown's oppressive thrall."

"Your loyalty is but a shroud,
For greed and power, you are proud.
The people's voice, you seek to quell,
In liberty's name, we'll break your spell."

Thomas Hutchinson:

"Your revolution breeds only strife,
It tears apart the fabric of life.

The crown provides a guiding light,
Against your chaos, we must fight."

"You speak of freedom, yet you blind,
With words that twist, and snares that bind.
The crown's command is wise and just,
In loyalty, we place our trust."

Together:

In tavern's gloom, their voices clash,
With words like lightning, tempers flash.
Two visions of a future bright,
Locked in a tavern's heated night.

Their arguments, both fierce and grand,
Echoed through the tavern's stand.
In every shout, in every plea,
The fate of nations fought to be.

78

Barkeep and Anglican in a Tavern

Barkeep and Anglican in a Tavern

In a tavern's warmth where shadows blend,
A barkeep and an Anglican defend,
Their differing views, their hearts laid bare,
In conversation rich with care.

Barkeep:

"Beneath this roof, all voices blend,
I serve the ale, I hear, I tend.
Yet lately, whispers fill the air,
Of freedom's call, of bold despair."

"The colonists, they seek to break,

From England's hold, for liberty's sake.
In every cup, in every cheer,
I feel the pulse of rising fear."

Anglican:

The Anglican, with collar neat,
Replied with voice so calm, discreet,
"Our church, our crown, we hold so dear,
In faith and loyalty, we steer."

"In sacred halls, we find our peace,
In England's grace, our bonds don't cease.
The rebels' cause, though fierce and bright,
Disrupts the order, fuels the fight."

Barkeep:

"Yet in this tavern, day by day,
I see the toll the taxes lay.
On common folk, who seek relief,
From tyranny's unending grief."

"Is it so wrong to seek a way,
Where freedom's light will guide the day?
To break the chains that bind so tight,
And forge a future, clear and bright?"

Anglican:

"Our faith, our crown, they guide us well,
In England's arms, we safely dwell.

The rebels' path, though paved with fire,
May lead to chaos, dark and dire."

"We pray for peace, for order's hand,
For unity across the land.
In church's light, we find our way,
In loyal grace, we choose to stay."

Together:

In tavern's glow, their voices blend,
A barkeep and an Anglican defend.
With ale in hand and faith in heart,
They share their worlds, though worlds apart.

The barkeep's dreams of freedom's cheer,
The Anglican's call for order dear,
In every word, a nation's fight,
Reflected in the tavern's light.

79

The Shadow of Empire: The French and Indian War

The Shadow of Empire: The French and Indian War

In forests dense where shadows creep,
And ancient trees their secrets keep,
The drums of war, a thunderous call,
Echo through the woodland's sprawl.

The Frenchmen bold, with allies near,
The native tribes, their hearts sincere,
In alliance dark, they stand as one,
'Neath the northern sun.

The British troops, with redcoats bright,
March onward through the darkened night,
To claim the land, to stake their claim,

In empire's name, in glory's fame.

The battles rage in forest deep,
Where spirits of the woodland weep,
At bloodshed wrought by stranger's hands,
In ancient, sacred, native lands.

From Fort Duquesne to Quebec's crest,
The soldiers fought, they gave their best,
Through winter's chill and summer's blaze,
In war's consuming, fiery gaze.

The native tribes, their spirits torn,
Between two fires, forlorn,
Their lands a prize in conqueror's eyes,
Their fate decided 'neath foreign skies.

Oh, war of shadows, war of might,
In history's scroll, your tales ignite,
The seeds of revolution sown,
In every battle, every groan.

For from this war, a spark did light,
A future bright, a freedom's fight,
The colonies, their voice found clear,
In independence, drawing near.

The French and Indian War's dark trail,
Through history's veil, its echoes wail,
A prelude to a greater fight,
For liberty, for justice's light.

80

The Proclamation of 1763

The Proclamation of 1763

In aftermath of war's dark blaze,
Where forest shadows hide the days,
A proclamation, cold decree,
From distant throne, across the sea.

Upon the parchment, lines are drawn,
From Appalachian dusk to dawn,
A boundary set, a king's command,
To halt the westward-moving hand.

"Here ye shall not pass," it cries,
"Where native lands 'neath western skies
Are held in sacred, ancient trust,
Protected from the settlers' thrust."

The colonists, with dreams so bright,
Of fertile fields, of open night,
Their hopes are dashed upon the line,
By royal edict's stern design.

The native tribes, in cautious cheer,
See in the law, a future clear,
Yet know the fickle hearts of men,
And fear the breaking of the pen.

Through taverns' murmur, in the streets,
The colonists with anger meet,
"Our rights, our land, by toil won,
Are shackled by this foreign crown."

In whispers low and voices loud,
In every restless, gathering crowd,
The seeds of discontent are sown,
In proclamation's heavy tone.

The year of seventeen sixty-three,
A line was drawn from sea to sea,
But in its shadow, fires ignite,
A future born of brewing fight.

For every line that history draws,
Is met with challenge, questioned laws,
The proclamation's stern decree,
A step toward the fight for liberty.

In royal halls, they could not see,
The storm that brewed, the destiny,

Of colonies that sought to be,
Forever bound, forever free.

81

The Sugar Act

The Sugar Act

In seventeen sixty-four's bright dawn,
A shadow cast, a burden drawn,
The Sugar Act, with taxes tight,
Imposed by Britain's distant might.

The molasses trade, so sweet and fair,
Now burdened with a tariff's snare,
From islands warm, where sugar cane
Grew tall beneath the tropic rain.

The merchants groaned, the traders cried,
As duties steep on goods were tied,
Their profits clipped by England's hand,
A distant rule they could not stand.

In Boston's ports, in Charleston's quay,
The whispers rose, a fervent plea,
"Unjust this tax, without our say,
The crown's decree, we must allay."

The Sugar Act, a bitter taste,
In colonists, a growing haste,
To challenge power, to seek redress,
Against the weight of king's impress.

Through taverns filled with discontent,
The seeds of revolution sent,
In pamphlets bold and speeches grand,
They called for justice in the land.

"No taxation without our voice,"
Became the rallying cry, the choice,
Of those who saw in every act,
A step toward liberty's contract.

The Sugar Act, though but a spark,
Ignited flames within the dark,
Of minds that dreamed of freedom's way,
And yearned to break the crown's array.

In history's scroll, its mark is clear,
A prelude to the rising cheer,
Of revolution's bold advance,
For freedom's dance, for independence.

Thus, in the annals, let it stand,
The Sugar Act's unyielding hand,

A catalyst for future bright,
In struggle's dawn, in freedom's light.

82

The Stamp Act

The Stamp Act

In the year of seventeen sixty-five,
A shadow deep began to thrive,
The Stamp Act, wrought by distant crown,
Upon the colonies, weighed down.

On paper, parchment, cards, and dice,
A tax imposed, a heavy price,
Each document and legal plea,
Bore the mark of tyranny.

The colonists, with righteous ire,
Spoke out against this unjust fire,
"No taxation without consent,"
Their rallying cry, their firmament.

In taverns filled with fervent talk,
In bustling streets where patriots walk,
The seeds of revolution sown,
In every heart, a discontent grown.

In Boston's streets and Philly's square,
The voices rose in heated air,
The Sons of Liberty took their stand,
To wrest control from England's hand.

The press, the courts, the merchant's stall,
All felt the weight of this new pall,
The stamped papers, a bitter sight,
In every home, in every light.

John Adams, with his quill in hand,
Denounced the tax across the land,
In pamphlets sharp, in speeches clear,
He voiced the rising, growing fear.

Patrick Henry's fiery speech,
In Virginia's halls did reach,
A fervor that would not be tamed,
A cry for rights, for freedom claimed.

Across the colonies, a wave,
Of unity, the bold and brave,
Petitions sent, assemblies called,
The Stamp Act's power thus forestalled.

The protests grew, the crown relented,
The tax repealed, the colonies contented,

But in the wake, a lesson learned,
The fires of freedom brightly burned.

The Stamp Act, in its heavy hand,
Brought forth a united stand,
A step along the path so vast,
Toward liberty, achieved at last.

83

The Stamp Act Congress

The Stamp Act Congress

In seventeen sixty-five's grim year,
A gathering bold, dispelled the fear,
In New York's city, delegates met,
To challenge Britain's harshest threat.

The colonies, in unity,
Sent forth their men with liberty,
From Massachusetts' steadfast shore,
To Georgia's fields, their voices bore.

Around the table, hearts aligned,
In common cause, their fates entwined,
The Stamp Act's weight, a burden shared,
By every voice that freedom dared.

With John Dickinson's eloquent pen,
They crafted words that rallied men,
Petitions sent to England's throne,
Demanding rights as fully grown.

"No taxation without our voice,"
In every heart became the choice,
A declaration firm and just,
To break the crown's oppressive thrust.

Their grievances, with reason laid,
In fervent tones, their stance displayed,
Against the Stamp Act's cruel demand,
They sought to free their troubled land.

Through heated debate and fervent plea,
They forged a path for liberty,
A congress born of common strife,
A step toward a freer life.

In taverns dark and halls so grand,
The echoes spread across the land,
The Stamp Act Congress, brave and true,
In history's scroll, a vision new.

For in their unity, they found,
The strength to stand on common ground,
A precursor to revolution's flame,
A legacy in freedom's name.

In New York's bustling, vibrant heart,
The colonies took their first bold start,

Toward a future, bright and clear,
Where every voice might have its cheer.

The Stamp Act Congress, thus renowned,
In unity, their cause was found,
A testament to freedom's fight,
In history's ever-burning light.

84

The Bitter Cup: A Townshend Tale

The Bitter Cup: A Townshend Tale

A shadow falls across the land,
A bitter draught, by Parliament's hand.
The Townshend Acts, a serpent's coil,
Tightening on freedoms, steeped in toil.

Taxes on tea, on glass, and paint,
A mocking grin, a searing taunt.
"No say in laws," the colonists cry,
"For what we earn, beneath a foreign sky?"

In Boston's streets, a silent rage,
A smoldering ember on history's page.
The Sons of Liberty, with whispers laced,

Plan acts of defiance, a bitter taste.

Boycotts erupt, a fiery chain,
Rejecting goods, a pouring rain
Of discontent, on British shores,
Echoing the discontent that forever roars.

The crown unyielding, tensions mount,
A fragile peace, with doubt's account.
The Townshend Acts, a spark ignite,
Fueling the flames of a coming fight.

85

The Streets Run Red: A Boston Ballad

The Streets Run Red: A Boston Ballad

Cobblestones slick with crimson rain,
A winter's eve, etched deep in pain.
A lone sentry, a taunting cry,
A spark ignited, beneath a leaden sky.

The crowd encroaches, a restless tide,
Words turn to blows, nowhere to hide.
Bricks and stones, a hurled command,
Soldiers surrounded, on hostile land.

A shot rings out, a startled call,
Echoes of chaos, consume them all.
Panic and fury, a bloody fray,

Innocent lives, forfeit the day.

Five souls lie silent, beneath the gaslight's glare,
A chilling tableau, etched in despair.
Propaganda's pen, with words aflame,
"Massacre!" they cry, whispering freedom's name.

The seeds of rebellion, firmly sown,
In fertile ground, where anger's grown.
The Boston Massacre, a haunting sight,
A crimson stain on liberty's fight.

86

Whispers on the Wind: A Committee's Call

Whispers on the Wind: A Committee's Call

In shadowed rooms, where candles gleam,
No grand display, no outward show,
But whispers carried, soft and low.
The Committee of Correspondence, a web unseen,

Threads of dissent, across the colonies keen.
Samuel Adams, a name whispered in fear,
Planting the seeds, a revolution near.
Pen and quill, their weapons of choice,

Spreading the message, with urgent voice.
Of grievances mounting, taxes unfair,
A crown's control, a burden to bear.

From town to town, the message takes flight,

Riders on horseback, cloaked in the night.
Sharing the news, of liberty's plight,
A call to unity, to defend their right.
In taverns and churches, the letters are read,

Kindling the flames, a righteous seed.
A network of whispers, a growing unrest,
The colonists stirring, from slumber's arrest.
The crown may not see, their plans unfold,

But whispers on the wind, a story untold.
The Committee of Correspondence, a force unbound,
A symphony of dissent, with a revolutionary sound.

87

The Smuggler's Moon: A Tea Act Tale

The Smuggler's Moon: A Tea Act Tale

A silver disc, a watchful eye,
Hangs heavy in the veiled night sky.
Beneath its glow, on ocean's crest,
A ship arrives, a dubious guest.

The East India Company, with greed untold,
Dumps mountains of tea, for a price of gold.
But shadows lurk, in harbor's hold,
Where whispers of defiance, turn frosty and bold.

The Townshend duty, a bitter pill,
A crown's decree, that makes freedom ill.
Dutch tea smuggled, a cheaper thrill,

Keeps colonists' coffers, comfortably filled.

The Tea Act's promise, a tempting snare,
Lowered prices, but a hidden dare.
A monopoly formed, a crown's control,
Infringing on freedoms, taking their toll.

In Boston's heart, a fire ignites,
Sons of Liberty, shrouded in night.
Mohawk's guise, a fierce disguise,
Dumping the cargo, beneath freedom's cries.

The moonbeams dance, on shattered leaves,
A protest enacted, the ocean grieves.
The Tea Act's folly, a king's decree,
Sparks revolution, for all to see.

88

The Tempestuous Night: A Boston Tea Party Ballad

The Tempestuous Night: A Boston Tea Party Ballad

The Boston Harbor, veiled in mist,
A restless slumber, the colonists kissed.
Three ships anchored, a cargo so grand,
Tea leaves from China, by a monarch's hand.

The Tea Act's burden, a bitter brew,
Taxation without say, a piercing hue.
"No representation!" the colonists cried,
Their anger simmering, deep inside.

On December's eve, with the moon as their guide,
A band of patriots, with righteous stride.
Mohawk disguises, a flickering flame,

Sons of Liberty, whispering their name.

Hatchets and crowbars, their tools of dissent,
Boarding the vessels, with resolute intent.
Into the deep, with a thunderous crash,
Tea chests they cast, with a fiery splash.

Three hundred forty-two, a symbolic plight,
A tempestuous night, bathed in pale moonlight.
A message delivered, with defiance bold,
"We will not be burdened, by stories untold!"

The crown enraged, with retribution's might,
But a fire ignited, burning ever so bright.
The Boston Tea Party, a turning point's fray,
A nation's spirit, awakened that day.

89

The Chains of Coercion: An Intolerable Tale

The Chains of Coercion: An Intolerable Tale

A fist of power, across the waves,
The Intolerable Acts, in freedom's grave.
Four laws descend, with cruel design,
To punish Boston, for a tea party's shine.

The Boston Port Act, a harbor sealed tight,
No commerce allowed, beneath the day's light.
Massachusetts' charter, ripped and torn,
Self-government's dream, forever forlorn.

Trials removed, a mockery of right,
Accused shipped away, for a foreign court's might.
Soldiers quartered, a burden untold,

Citizens' homes, turned bitter and cold.

Quebec appeased, with a faith divide,
Further inflaming the colonies' pride.
A web of control, a tyrant's decree,
But the spirit of freedom, refused to be free.

From colony to colony, the outrage did spread,
A united front, where defiance was bred.
The First Continental Congress, a flame alight,
To challenge the crown, and defend their birthright.

The Intolerable Acts, a miscalculation's sting,
Fueling the fire, a revolution's wing.
For every act of force, a rebellion's embrace,
The colonists rising, to claim their rightful place.

90

In Carpenter's Hall: A Congress of Voices

In Carpenter's Hall: A Congress of Voices

In Philadelphia's heart, a hall of wood,
Gathered delegates, misunderstood.
Thirteen colonies, a patchwork spread,
Whispers of unity, unspoken dread.

From fiery Adams, to Washington's might,
Each voice a faction, in freedom's flickering light.
Moderates plead, for reason's gentle hold,
While radicals simmer, with stories untold.

Boycotts debated, a weapon to wield,
Against British grandeur, on a distant field.
The weight of dependence, a crown's heavy hand,

Taxation's injustice, across the land.

Days turned to weeks, beneath the watchful eye,
Of portraits stern, gazing from on high.
Compromise forged, a fragile line,
A united front, for a cause divine.

The First Continental Congress, a hesitant start,
A bridge of defiance, mending a broken heart.
No revolution declared, no swords yet drawn,
But a seed of rebellion, firmly sown.

Letters dispatched, a message to send,
The crown's demands, they would not bend.
A Second Congress planned, a fateful decree,
The murmurs of revolution, for all to see.

91

❦

The Shot Heard Round the World: A Lexington Ballad

The Shot Heard Round the World: A Lexington Ballad

A hush descends on Lexington Green,
Where farmers gather, a peaceful scene.
Musket butts grounded, a nervous wait,
For rumors of redcoats, sealing their fate.

Paul Revere rides, a legend in flight,
"The British are coming!" a desperate cry in the night.
From slumber roused, the minutemen rise,
A call to defend, beneath freedom's skies.

At dawn's first light, a scarlet tide,
British troops march, with nowhere to hide.
A captain's order, a voice so bold,

"Disperse, ye rebels, or stories unfold!"

A spark ignites, a musket's call,
Confusion reigns, through the gathering squall.
Eight men lie fallen, on Lexington Green,
The fight for freedom, a brutal scene.

Onward they march, to Concord they press,
Where hidden stores, the colonists possess.
But by the North Bridge, a stand they make,
Minutemen gather, for liberty's sake.

A volley erupts, from hidden hand,
British retreat, across the land.
The countryside roused, a hornet's nest,
Militia swarms, putting redcoats to the test.

From Lexington Green, to Concord's embrace,
A revolution sparked, at a fateful pace.
The "shot heard round the world," a turning tide,
A nation awakened, with nowhere to hide.

92

In Liberty's Cradle: A Second Congress Convenes

In Liberty's Cradle: A Second Congress Convenes

Philadelphia stirs, with a nation's weight,
The Second Congress, sealed by destiny's fate.
Delegates gather, from colonies bold,
Whispers of revolution, slowly unfold.

No longer pleas, for a king's embrace,
But murmurs of defiance, etched on each face.
Washington ascends, a leader born,
To guide the colonies, through battles yet sworn.

John Adams' fire, and Franklin's wit,
Forge a new path, where freedom can't be quit.
The Olive Branch Petition, a final plea,

But King George unyielding, blind as can be.

The Continental Army, a fledgling band,
Against a mighty force, they make their stand.
Paper money printed, a gamble they take,
To fund the rebellion, for liberty's sake.

Debate and dissent, in candlelit halls,
The question of unity, echoes through walls.
But independence whispers, a growing desire,
To break the chains, and set their nation on fire.

The Second Continental Congress, a crucible's hold,
Transforming colonies, into a story untold.
A nation in its cradle, taking its first breath,
Ready to fight for freedom, or face certain death.

93

The Unsung Plea: An Olive Branch's Lament

The Unsung Plea: An Olive Branch's Lament

Across the waves, a parchment takes flight,
An olive branch offered, bathed in pale moonlight.
The Second Congress, with hearts full of dread,
A final entreaty, for peace to be spread.

John Dickinson's quill, a plea so sincere,
Appealing to kinship, a bond held so dear.
"We are still your subjects," the petition cried,
"Let grievances mend, before all is defied."

Memories of battles, a simmering rage,
Yet hope flickered faintly, turning history's page.
Taxes and laws, the colonists plead,

A chance for reconciliation, a desperate need.

But deaf fell the ears, across the ocean wide,
The King saw rebellion, where loyalty did hide.
The petition unread, a symbol cast down,
The flames of revolution, burning all around.

In dusty archives, the parchment now lies,
A forgotten plea, beneath freedom's cries.
The Olive Branch Petition, a story untold,
A wish for peace, forever left cold.

94

When Tyranny Unchains: A Declaration's Decree

When Tyranny Unchains: A Declaration's Decree

When human bonds, by harsh decree,
Must sever ties, and yearn to be
Free and independent, nature's call,
Demands a statement, heard by all.

With decent respect, to world opinion's ear,
We, colonies united, cast off fear.
A history etched, of wrongs endured,
A king's abuses, forever assured.

The right to life, to liberty's embrace,
The pursuit of happiness, a sacred space.
These truths self-evident, by Heaven's hand,

No king can extinguish, across the land.

Governments derive their just powers,
From the consent of the governed, through the hours.
When a ruler destroys, and rights infringe,
It's the people's right, the tyrant to unhinge.

A long train of abuses, a litany of pain,
Unveils a pattern, a despotic reign.
Taxes imposed, without a voice,
Representation denied, a stifled choice.

We've petitioned humbly, for justice to mend,
But pleas unanswered, a story without end.
We warn the world, of a tyrant's might,
And declare ourselves, free and in the right.

With firm reliance, on Divine Providence,
We pledge our lives, our fortunes, sacred essence.
The unanimous declaration, for all to see,
These United States, forever to be free.

95

A nation's spirit, taking flight.

A Nation Forged: A Ballad of Revolution's Fire

Across the waves, a discontent did spread,
Thirteen colonies, where shadows tread.
Townshend Acts' burden, a bitter pill,
"No taxation," their growing will.

The Boston Massacre, a crimson stain,
Spark ignited, whispers of disdain.
Committees formed, with whispers laced,
A web of defiance, a message embraced.

The Tea Act's folly, a king's decree,
Dumped in the harbor, for all to see.
The Boston Tea Party, a tempestuous night,

A nation's spirit, taking flight.

The Intolerable Acts, a tyrant's sting,
Further inflamed, a revolution's wing.
The First Congress formed, a fragile thread,
Unity sought, where defiance spread.

At Lexington Green, the "shot heard round the world,"
Minutemen gathered, a story unfurled.
Concord's embrace, a battle's cry,
Redcoats retreating, beneath a freedom-filled sky.

The Second Congress, a nation's hold,
Washington leading, a story untold.
The Olive Branch offered, a final plea,
But deaf fell the ears, across the rolling sea.

The Declaration's thunder, a glorious sound,
"Free and independent," on hallowed ground.
With life, fortune, and sacred honor sworn,
A new nation birthed, a revolutionary morn.

Valley Forge's winter, a test of might,
Soldiers enduring, beneath the starlit night.
Yorktown's surrender, a victory won,
But freedom's cost, beneath a setting sun.

From revolution's embers, a phoenix arose,
The United States, where liberty flows.
A testament etched, in history's grand design,
A nation forged, forever to shine.

96

The Great Molasses Flood
of Boston, 1919

The Great Molasses Flood of Boston, 1919

O, City of Boston, cradle of liberty,
Hear now the tale, the strange, ghastly tale,
Of the day when sweet molasses turned to doom,
When the streets flowed thick with death.

It was January's unexpected warmth,
A day when winter's breath turned mild,
And the rusted tank, filled to its brim,
Held two million gallons of sticky life.

At Copp's Hill, it stood, old and leaking,
A monstrous vat, groaning with its burden,
Until at noon, the fates conspired,

And metal rivets, like shrapnel, flew.

The tank erupted, a beast unchained,
Its molten innards thrust into the air,
With force enough to fell the steel,
And crush the buildings in its path.

A wall of goo, thirty feet high,
Rushed down the cobbled streets,
At a speed that mocked the wind,
Carrying with it chaos and despair.

Molasses, sweet and slow in memory,
Now a torrent, dark and wild,
Swept all before it—people, horses,
Homes and dreams alike, submerged.

Through Commercial Street it roared,
A sticky tide that claimed its due,
Drowning cries, silencing the day,
In a layer thick, two to three feet deep.

Rescue came but struggled too,
For even heroes stuck in goo,
As Boston wept, the sweetness turned,
To a sorrow deep, a lesson learned.

Molasses, residue of sugar's toil,
Once destined for rum, for cattle, for munitions,
Now a grave, a sticky tomb,
For twenty-one souls, lost too soon.

O, hear the echoes of their plight,
In the whispers of the summer breeze,
When Boston's heat revives the scent,
Of that fateful day, long past.

This flood, this dark and bitter flood,
A reminder of industry's cost,
When greed and carelessness entwine,
And lives are lost in sweet deceit.

So, raise a glass, remember well,
The Great Molasses Flood's dread tale,
A chapter strange in Boston's lore,
Where liberty's cradle faced a sticky end.

97

The Great Molasses Flood
of 1919

The Great Molasses Flood of 1919

In Boston town where shadows fell,
A tale of dread we now must tell,
Of sweetness turned to deadly tide,
When molasses flowed with vengeful pride.

On January's midmost day,
The sun's rare warmth held dark at bay,
Yet in the North End's bustling heart,
A monstrous fate would soon impart.

A tank, immense and rusting sore,
Held sweetened death behind its door,
Two million gallons, dark and thick,

Of molasses, brewed in cauldron's slick.

At noon, the tank could bear no more,
It burst with roar, a thunderous score,
Steel rivets flew, like shrapnel cast,
Through girders strong, through moments past.

A vacuum's force, a chilling gasp,
As buildings crumbled in its clasp,
A truck was dragged, a train derailed,
As chaos reigned and terror hailed.

Then down Commercial Street it came,
A wall of goo, a deadly claim,
Thirty feet high, and fierce it sped,
Like demon's breath, in shadows spread.

The neighborhood, in horror steeped,
As molasses dark, through windows seeped,
It buried men, and beasts alike,
In sticky grasp, in mortal strike.

The cries of children, muffled, lost,
In treacle's grip, their lives were tossed,
Rescuers trapped in syrup's bind,
A scene of dread, of horrors lined.

Sweet residue of sugar's toil,
Now turned to death in sticky coil,
A flood that claimed both life and breath,
A city's heart now marred by death.

The streets were stained, the air was thick,
With sorrow's scent, with doom's bleak trick,
And even now, on summer's day,
The ghostly smell won't fade away.

A plaque alone, in Puopolo's park,
Remembers well that fateful dark,
The Great Molasses Flood of yore,
A tragic tale forevermore.

In Boston's history, shadows cast,
A moment where the sweetness passed,
Into the realm of ghastly lore,
Where syrup's tide was stained with gore.

98

The Great Chicago Fire

The Great Chicago Fire

In autumn's dusk of '71,
A blaze begun, a nightmare spun,
In O'Leary's barn, the spark was cast,
And Chicago's fate was sealed, so vast.

A windy night, the flames took flight,
A city's heart was wrapped in blight,
Through wooden streets and tindered homes,
The fire roared, the demon roams.

Four miles long, a mile wide,
The inferno spread with ruthless stride,
The buildings fell, the streets were lost,
In flames that came with deadly cost.

Three hundred souls to flames consigned,
Ninety thousand left behind,
Homeless, wandering through the night,
Seeking refuge from the fright.

The Waterworks, the city's pride,
Succumbed to fire's relentless tide,
A burning ember's fatal kiss,
Turned water's hope to dark abyss.

Fire devils danced in heated air,
Their fiery breath spread dread and scare,
Buildings once proud, now crumbled, charred,
A city's dream, so deeply marred.

Yet from the ashes, hope was born,
In tears and sweat of mourning's morn,
The Great Rebuilding then began,
With stone and brick, with iron's span.

No longer wood, but mortar strong,
The city rose, with iron song,
New laws decreed a fireproof age,
Chicago turned a golden page.

The Palmer House, with clay and sand,
Stood as a testament, so grand,
To terra cotta's saving grace,
A fortress in the fire's place.

The Montauk Block reached to the sky,
With clay tiles keeping spirits high,

And from the fire's grim demise,
The first skyscrapers dared to rise.

The Chicago School, in steel and light,
Brought forth a future, bold and bright,
With Sullivan, Burnham, and their kin,
They built anew, with strength within.

In LaSalle Street, a tower grew,
The Home Insurance Building, new,
With steel cage frame and windows wide,
It stood a beacon, city's pride.

Thus, through the flames and smoke and tears,
Chicago rose across the years,
A testament to human will,
To build anew, to dream, to fill.

The Great Chicago Fire's fierce dance,
Brought death and loss, yet gave the chance,
To rise again from fiery grave,
In strength and hope, the city brave.

99

Peshtigo Fire

Peshtigo Fire

Hark! A tale of woe from Wisconsin's heart,
Where flames of fury tore a land apart.
Eighteenth of October, bathed in autumn's glow,
A fiery serpent writhed, unleashing woe.

Dryness held the land in choking grip,
Man's hand had wrought the forests to a chip.
Logs and leaves, a tinderbox they lay,
Awaiting spark to ignite the coming fray.

Then rose the wind, a demon from the west,
With bellows strong, it fanned the smoldering crest.
A fiery maw, agape and hungering deep,
Consumed the earth, while mortals cried and shrieked.

Peshtigo, fair town, to cinders turned,
No refuge found, as homes and hopes all burned.
Families scattered, lost in smoke's embrace,
Loved ones vanished, leaving naught a trace.

Brave Kelly sought his kin, through smoke and night,
One child he held, a beacon in the fight.
But wife and babes, where had they gone astray?
A cruel wind's jest, upon this woeful day.

Two children found, embraced in slumber deep,
Beside their burning home, where memories sleep.
A mother's tears, a lonely, mournful sound,
Amidst the wreckage, scattered all around.

A lesson learned, in fire's cruel light,
Respect the land, and hold its future tight.
For nature's wrath, unleashed by careless hand,
Can leave a scar upon a ravaged land.

Though flames may rise, and forests fall anew,
May knowledge guide us, ever strong and true.
With weather's aid, and wisdom's guiding hand,
Such tragedies may never scorch the land.

From Erin's shores, where verdant pastures lie,
The Faithful Stewart set her sails on high.
A gallant bark, with two hundred seventy souls,
Bound for fair Philadelphia's distant goals.

Four hundred casks, with gleaming copper fraught,
Her precious cargo, dearly bought and sought.

For fifty-three long days, on ocean's breast,
She braved the waves, and Neptune's harsh behest.

But cruel the Fates, their purpose unforeseen,
Off Delaware's coast, a shoal, a watery scene.
Cape Henlopen's grasp, a treacherous embrace,
Stranded the ship, in dire and dismal case.

Though near the shore, a tantalizing sight,
No watchful guard to guide them through the night.
No lifeguard's hand, to snatch them from the deep,
Alone they faced the fury, while men did weep.

With broken spars, and timbers rent and torn,
They built their rafts, a forlorn hope, forlorn.
The raging sea, a relentless, hungry beast,
Claimed countless lives, a cruel and savage feast.

By morning's light, a tragic scene unfurled,
One hundred eighty-one, lost to the world.
Just sixty-eight remained, with hearts that bled,
The Faithful Stewart, on that shoal, lay dead.

Her bones now scattered, where the breakers foam,
A monument to lives that found no home.
But Coin Beach whispers, of the treasure lost,
Where copper gleams, at tempest's heavy cost.

A tale of woe, for bards to ever sing,
Of human frailty, and the ocean's sting.
May watchful eyes, on future shores reside,
Lest such a fate, befall another tide.

100

The Shuddering of San Francisco

The Shuddering of San Francisco

Once upon a morn unbroken, in the pale dawn's early yawn,
Came a shiver, came a tremor, came a quaking to the town.
Jesse Cook, the sergeant stalwart, stood with strangers, faces drawn,
Watching, waiting, hearts a-thudding, for the earth to settle down.
Seconds stretched to years of terror, shadows deepening to drown,
Lives collapsing, hopes unspun, amid the chaos, dark and brown.

As the trembling ceased its clamor, silence fell like phantom's pall,
Hundreds, lifeless, lay in ruin, dreams extinguished in their thrall.

Flimsy lodgings, stacked like kindling, crumbled, sank, and buried all,
Water mains beneath the cobbles, shattered, severed, beyond call.
Wires tangled, signals dying, in the early morning sprawl,
For the city, known and loved, had answered fate's relentless call.

Flames ignited, swiftly spreading, turning wood to cinders bright,
Brushfire fury, block to block, engulfing all within its sight.
Survivors fled, their treasures hoarded, in the chaos of the night,
Smoke asphyxiating trapped ones, flames consuming with their might.
Firefighters, desperate, hurried, battling blaze in futile fight,
Drawing water from the trickles, as the winds fanned flames alight.

News of horror, swiftly traveled, faster than it e'er had done,
Wireless signals, telegraphing, spoke of terror 'neath the sun.
Pictures vivid, stark in contrast, showing towers overrun,
Captured hearts and minds of many, as the tale of woe begun.
A nation watched in somber silence, gripped by fear, by sorrow spun,
Witnessing the mighty city, humbled, broken, and undone.

When the flames had spent their anger, when the ashes cooled and stilled,
San Francisco lay in ruins, shadows of a past fulfilled.
Churches crumbled, homes demolished, dreams and hopes for-ever killed,
Every street a tale of mourning, every heart with sorrow filled.
Yet within the smoldering embers, tales of hope began to build,
"From these ashes, grander rises," cried the city, iron-willed.

Years would pass, and in their passing, headlines told of rebirth's
glow,
Buildings rising, streets returning, life emerging from the woe.
But beneath the fervent stories, deeper truths began to show,
Of the lives forever altered, of the pain we scarcely know.
"1906" became the whisper, of a grief both loud and low,
Marking time between the ages, where the present meets the
long ago.

Thus in numbers, cold and telling, history's voice begins to fade,
Measured by the scale of loss, by the memories left in shade.
Seismographs and geologists, in their data, have portrayed
The tremor's wrath, the earth's great fissure, where the ancient
fault is laid.
Yet within the hearts of many, echoes of the past invade,
Whispering of the shuddered morning, of the dues that fate
has paid.

San Francisco, phoenix city, rising from its ashen grave,
Holds within its stones a story, of the bold and of the brave.
Though the scars of old disasters in the past may still enslave,
Every year the city gathers, memories, as waves, do wave.
"1906" they speak in reverence, of the lives they fought to save,
Echoes of a haunting morning, resting in the past's dark cave.

The Great San Francisco Earthquake and Fire

The Great San Francisco Earthquake and Fire

In April's dawn, the earth did groan,
San Francisco, pride and throne,
Shuddered 'neath the fault's cruel hand,
A nightmare none could understand.

The year was nineteen hundred six,
A tremor struck, the ground affixed,
With violent shake, a fractured might,
The San Andreas roared its spite.

Two hundred seventy miles did break,
A rift that left the earth to quake,
The city quivered, structures fell,

As nature's wrath cast its dark spell.

A magnitude of seven-nine,
The seismograph's despairing line,
Recorded at Chabot's great dome,
The trembling heart of many a home.

The earth did split, the buildings caved,
The streets of gold were now enslaved,
To fire's breath, to hellish glow,
A city lost in flames' cruel show.

The quake was but the opening act,
For fire swept with fierce impact,
Through alleys, streets, and houses grand,
A blaze unquenched by human hand.

Three days and nights, the fire did reign,
O'er fallen stones and ashen plain,
Three hundred thousand souls displaced,
Their city's glory now erased.

The Ferry Building stood in woe,
The State Mining Bureau's throes,
Surveyors' focus turned to dust,
As minerals lost their gilded trust.

No maps of faults, no seismograph,
Could halt the quake's infernal wrath,
The study of the earth's great seams,
Lay dormant in their hopeful dreams.

Yet from the ruins, knowledge grew,
A quest for truth, for science new,
To understand the fault's cruel game,
And guard against the earth's fierce claim.

The Geological Survey rose,
To map the faults, to diagnose,
The tremors of a restless land,
To comprehend, to understand.

In memory of that April day,
When earth and fire had their way,
We've learned to watch, to heed the signs,
To read the faults, the hidden lines.

For every quake's anniversary,
We ponder on the mystery,
Of nature's power, raw and wild,
And how to guard each precious child.

The Great San Francisco Earthquake taught,
That knowledge gained is dearly bought,
And though we build and though we plan,
We bow before earth's mighty hand.

The Dam is Becoming Dangerous and May Possibly Go!

The Dam is Becoming Dangerous and May Possibly Go!

Behold the hour, when shadows darken skies,
And direful whispers on the zephyrs rise,
The South Fork Dam, in perilous might,
Doth threaten doom, and breeds a fearful night.

On that fateful Friday, in May's tender bloom,
The heavens wept, foretelling grievous gloom,
The waters swelled, and fate, in cruel jest,
Unleashed its wrath, from mountain's lofty crest.

Twenty million tons, a monstrous tide,

Did from its bonds in furious release glide,
Down the vale, with relentless force it sped,
A monstrous wave, to leave a town in dread.

Johnstown, fair Johnstown, in that dreadful hour,
Felt nature's wrath, unleashed with grievous power,
Two thousand souls and more, in watery grave,
Their lives swept off, by that unbridled wave.

Families, whole lineages, swept aside,
Children and parents, no place to hide,
Their homes, their dreams, in moments rent asunder,
By the relentless force, that roared like thunder.

Ninety-nine families, now no more,
Three hundred and ninety-six children, life's breath tore,
Women and men, widowed by the score,
In the wake of waters, such sorrow bore.

Unknown and lost, seven hundred fifty souls,
Laid to rest in nameless, silent shoals,
Far as Cincinnati, in distant lands,
The flood's grim touch left death's demands.

From South Fork's heights, to Johnstown's stricken streets,
Fourteen miles, the grim tale repeats,
The dam, once proud, now a ruinous tale,
Of negligence, where man and nature pale.

Owned by those of stature, wealth, and pride,
Carnegie and Frick, their names allied,
But now their legacies, in grief do blend,

For nature's fury, heedeth not such men.

The wave, a giant thirty feet and more,
With speed unmatch'd, at forty miles it bore,
Swept locomotives, steel giants flung,
By force untamed, from waters, wild and young.

Yet in this tale of woe, a spark of light,
Clara Barton came, to ease the plight,
The Red Cross, in its noble first array,
Brought hope to those, where darkness held its sway.

From nations far, aid swiftly did arrive,
In brotherhood, mankind did strive,
To heal the wounds, of Johnstown's grievous fate,
And in compassion's light, their sorrows sate.

O let this tale remind us, evermore,
That in our hearts, compassion we restore,
To guard and cherish, life with all its ken,
And leave no act undone, for the preservation of our fellow men.

103

Valley Forge

Valley Forge

When icicles hang by the wall, and keen winds do blow,
Ere night's cloak doth fall, and morning brings naught but woe,
We find our noble warriors encamped in a vale of sorrow,
'Neath the cold, cruel sky, awaiting a brighter morrow.

Here, at Valley Forge, doth History's quill be writ,
In blood and frost, where frozen tears and valor sit.
No verdant spring, nor gentle zephyr's kiss,
Could lift the chill from this abysmal abyss.

Lo, our brave commanders, George, steadfast and true,
His spirit unwavering, his heart pure as dew,
Guiding with firm resolve, his weary, beleaguered men,
Through trials and tribulations, o'er mountain, moor, and fen.

The hours grow long, and provisions grow scant,
Each soldier's breath a ghostly chant.
In tatters, their uniforms speak tales of grief,
Yet in their hearts, doth burn belief.

Muskets lay silent, no clarion call of war,
Yet here the battle rages, within each soldier's core.
'Tis not a foe of flesh and blood they face,
But Nature's fierce onslaught, her cold embrace.

Hunger gnaws and sickness stalks the camp,
Their makeshift shelters offer naught but damp.
Yet, midst this cruel despair, a phoenix stirs,
The promise of liberty, their noble cause prefers.

Around the fires, their spirits gather close,
With tales of home, and dreams of bright morose.
In their eyes, a gleam, a hope that cannot die,
For Freedom's clarion call reaches to the sky.

Thus, from the forge of winter, hearts of steel are made,
In the crucible of suffering, their faith shall ne'er fade.
Valley Forge, thou art a testament of might,
Where darkness bred the dawn of Freedom's light.

Oh, ye who look upon this frozen glade,
Remember well the price that hath been paid.
For in this vale of sorrow, where courage did not cease,
The seeds were sown for our land's sweet release.

So let us sing of Valley Forge, in days both old and new,
A saga of endurance, where patriots' spirits grew.

In frost and fire, their legend shall remain,
A beacon of resolve, through hardship and through pain.

104

Crossing of the Delaware River

Crossing of the Delaware River

When night's velvet mantle enshrouded the land,
And the wintry breath of December did command,
A tale of valor and cunning doth unfold,
Of warriors bold, braving the tempest's cold.

The Delaware, a river broad and fierce,
With icy veins and depths that pierce,
Lay as a barrier 'twixt hope and despair,
Yet, 'twas there our tale of glory and grit would repair.

In the somber night, 'neath a starless sky,
Where the frigid winds and silence vie,
General George, with his steadfast gaze,

Did marshal his men through the wintry haze.

Row upon row, the soldiers did gather,
In fragile boats, through storm they would tether,
Each stroke a symphony of resolve and might,
Guided by stars, though hidden from sight.

The river's icy breath, a chilling embrace,
Tested their spirits, in this perilous race,
Yet through the gloom, with courage adorned,
They crossed the Delaware, where legends are born.

Their oars did beat a relentless refrain,
A testament to enduring pain,
The ice did crack, and waters did roar,
But Washington led, undaunted, to shore.

Across the treacherous tide, they silently swept,
While the Hessian foes in their slumber kept,
With dawn's first light, the battle did ignite,
A Christmas surprise, a reclaiming of might.

The foes, unprepared for the morning fray,
Found themselves ensnared in disarray,
For Washington's gambit, bold and grand,
Did breathe new life into this war-torn land.

Thus, from the icy depths of Delaware's flow,
A victory sprung, amidst frost and snow,
A beacon of hope in the darkest of night,
The crossing, a symbol of liberty's light.

Remember this tale, ye patriots all,
Of courage and faith that did not fall,
For in the crossing of that river wide,
The seeds of triumph and freedom reside.

105

A Wife's Lament:
Remember the Truth

A Wife's Lament: Remember the Truth

February's chill gripped Havana's air that day,
The USS Maine, a sleeping giant, anchored in the bay.
News trickled in, a muffled, monstrous boom,
The battleship in flames, a watery tomb.

My heart, it clenched, a wife's unending dread,
For William, my love, on board, with hundreds dead.
The papers screamed, with headlines bold and stark,
"Remember the Maine!" a nation left in the dark.

"Blame Spain!" they cried, a fiery, vengeful call,
Yet whispers lingered, casting doubt on all.
Was it a mine, an act of hidden hand?

Or some mishap, within the burning land

Of coal compartments, a fire's fierce embrace?
The truth obscured, in speculation's chase.
Two hundred forty-six, brave souls now gone,
Their families left, to mourn the battle won,

Not on the battlefield, but in a harbor's sleep,
A senseless loss, hearts heavy, eyes that weep.
For William, and the others, lost that day,
I pray for peace, the war drums held at bay.

Let reason guide us, not a thirst for blood,
Unravel truth, where shadows once have stood.
May justice find its voice, and vengeance cease,
A soldier's wife, I yearn for lasting peace.

106

American Spies of the Revolution

American Spies of the Revolution

Nathan Hale

In those dire hours when Liberty lay in jeopardy, arose a soul whose gallant spirit matched his fate. Amongst the host of valiant hearts that beat for freedom, one Nathan Hale, a captain in the Continental Army, did stand distinct. The tale of Hale's sacrifice is steeped in the noble hue of martyrdom. During the grim skirmishes of Long Island, he did volunteer, with ardent fervor, to traverse the enemy's shadows, cloaked in the guise of common guise, to glean the designs of British might. Alas, fortune turned its back, and the British caught him. On the twenty-second day of September, in the year 1776, Hale met his untimely end, yet his spirit soared, undaunted, to the annals of eternity with the poignant utterance: "I only regret that I have but one life to give for my country." Thus, he became a beacon of sacrifice, his legacy etched in the marble of freedom's lore.

Benjamin Tallmadge and the Culper Spy Ring

In the theatre of clandestine endeavors, Benjamin Tallmadge did emerge as a master of intrigue. Entrusted by the sage General George Washington, Tallmadge wrought the Culper Spy Ring in November 1778, amidst the perilous heart of New York City, the very stronghold of British dominion. His assembly of discreet informants was a tapestry woven with threads of trust and valor, each thread a testament to the cause of liberty. As the chief orchestrator, Tallmadge's oversight endured till the curtain of war fell, his network a silent, invisible hand steering the fate of a nascent nation.

The Men and Women of the Culper Spy Ring

Austin Roe

In the humble guise of a tavern owner, Austin Roe plied his trade not in ale alone but in secrets and whispers of the rebellion. A kin of Caleb Brewster by proximity and resolve, Roe bore the perilous mantle of courier, traversing from Robert Townsend's bustling coffee house in New York City to the quietude of Setauket, Long Island—a journey exceeding fifty miles. Each sojourn was fraught with danger, the specter of discovery ever looming, yet Roe persisted, a silent sentinel of the Patriot cause.

Abraham Woodhull

A farmer by vocation and the son of a Patriot judge, Abraham Woodhull did cast aside the plow for the pen of secrecy. Joining the Culper Ring in the chill of November 1778, Woodhull, under the nom de guerre "Samuel Culper Sr.," became the nerve center of the ring. With a discerning eye, he sifted through intelligence, transmitting the precious gleanings to reach the ear of General Washington, evading British detection with a dexterity born of cunning and courage.

Anna Strong

From the pastoral expanses of Long Island, Anna Strong wielded the quotidian tools of her homestead to signal her compatriots. Her clothesline became a cipher, its garments a covert lexicon, guiding Caleb Brewster to hidden messages. Strong, the spouse of Patriot judge Selah Strong III, navigated the perilous tightrope of espionage with grace, her farmstead a hub of clandestine operations.

Robert Townsend

In the bustling heart of New York, Robert Townsend played a dangerous masquerade, a Patriot heart masked by Loyalist semblance. As a tavern keeper and journalist for a Loyalist gazette, Townsend's ruse garnered him access to the innermost workings of the British, his secrets relayed through Austin Roe, furthering the cause he silently served.

The Unseen Heroes

James Armistead Lafayette

Beneath the yoke of bondage, James Armistead Lafayette did rise, a double agent in the employ of freedom. Feigning allegiance to the British as a runaway slave, Armistead infiltrated the camp of the infamous traitor Benedict Arnold and the formidable Lord Cornwallis. His reports, a crucial fulcrum in the balance of war, guided the American forces to a decisive triumph at Yorktown.

Ann Bates

Ann Bates, a schoolteacher of Philadelphia, donned the guise of Patriotism to aid the British cause. With a keen eye and sharp wit, Bates infiltrated the headquarters of George Washington at White Plains, her observations relayed to General Henry Clinton. Her espionage influenced strategic deployments, her deeds a stark reminder of the thin line betwixt loyalty and betrayal.

Thus, in the shadowy interplay of espionage, these valiant souls wove the threads of victory with their cunning and sacrifice. Their deeds, oft unsung, didst fortify the edifice of American liberty, their legacy a testament to the silent, enduring power of resolve.

107

The Silent Threads
of Liberty

The Silent Threads of Liberty

In shadows deep, where secrets weave,
The quiet souls who dared believe,
Wrought tales of valor, clandestine,
Where courage in the dark did shine.

Nathan Hale, with heart of flame,
To spy for freedom, knew the game.
In Long Island's veil, he trod alone,
The price he paid, his life disowned.
Captured, condemned, his voice a light,
"I regret but one life for this fight."

Benjamin Tallmadge, Washington's eye,

Wove the Culper's intricate spy.
With friends he trusted, tales unfurled,
Within the enemy's hidden world.
Secrets whispered through the night,
Guiding rebels to the fight.

Austin Roe, the tavern man,
On treacherous roads, his courage ran.
From Townsend's shop to Setauket's shore,
A courier of secrets, danger's core.
Fifty miles of peril's call,
With every step, the risk of fall.

Abraham Woodhull, farmer's guise,
In coded notes, his wisdom lies.
Samuel Culper, secret name,
Through subtle signs, he played the game.
With cunning wit, he led the ring,
Silent savior to the king.

Anna Strong, her laundry told,
In hanging clothes, secrets bold.
Signals sent through pegs and sheets,
To Brewster's eyes, a silent fleet.
Her husband's cause, she fortified,
With every cloth, the British spied.

Robert Townsend, Loyalist face,
In tavern's crowd, his heart a brace.
Patriot true, he feigned the foe,
In loyal words, the secrets flow.
To Roe he sent the guarded lines,

Hidden truth through hidden signs.

James Armistead, double guise,
From chains of fate, to freedom's prize.
As runaway slave, he fooled the red,
In Cornwallis' camp, their plans he read.
His tales of war, their downfall spelled,
In Yorktown's fight, his truth was held.

Ann Bates, a traitor's lore,
With British heart, the lines she wore.
Amongst the rebels, she did tread,
Their might, their strength, she quietly bled.
With notes of force, to Clinton's ears,
She swayed the tides, provoked their fears.

In twilight's cloak, these spirits rose,
To weave the threads of freedom's prose.
Their silent acts, the dawn of light,
Through shadow's depth, they turned the fight.
For liberty, they cast their lot,
In whispered deeds, their names forgot.

108

Beneath the Liberty Tree and Beyond

Beneath the Liberty Tree and Beyond

1. The Midnight Ride

A lone horseman streaks through the night, Hooves pounding a message of coming fight. Through slumbering towns, a spectral form, Bearing tidings that ignite the storm.

1. Echoes of Bunker Hill

The crimson stain upon the verdant height, A silent testament to freedom's fight. Ghosts of soldiers whisper in the breeze, Of valor's price, beneath the rustling trees.

1. Whispers from the Liberty Bell

A tolling tongue, a voice that calls, For liberty's flame to pierce the walls. In iron heart, a nation's plea, Forever etched, "Proclaim liberty!"

1. Ballad of the Loyalist

Torn loyalties, a heart in strife, Bound by duty, yet yearning for life. Whispers of treason, a shadowed face, Lost in the echoes of a changing race.

1. The Raven at Valley Forge

A tattered flag against the winter's bite, Soldiers huddled, through the starless night. A raven settles on a frosted gun, Its croaking voice, "Will freedom be won?"

1. Lexington Green by Dawn

The mist hangs heavy, where the redcoats fell, A silent grave-yard, where freedom's knell First shattered peace, a shot that rang, A nation's spirit, forever changed.

1. The Martyr's Pyre

Crackling flames lick at the midnight air, A silhouette hangs, a silent prayer. Betrayal's kiss, a hero's plight, Burning bright, in freedom's light.

1. The Hessian's Lament

Far from the homeland, a foreign shore, Fighting battles they don't understand anymore. A soldier's longing, a whispered plea, To return home, from this haunting sea.

1. Beneath the Liberty Tree

A gathering place, beneath the boughs so grand, Words of dissent, whispered and planned. Seeds of rebellion, taking root, A nation's yearning, bearing fruit.

1. The Witch of Salem and the Sons of Liberty

Whispers of discord, a town in fright, Accusations fly, beneath the pale moonlight. But freedom's spirit, it cannot be chained, Even by shadows, forever unclaimed.

1. Yorktown's Lament

The drumbeat fades, the cannons fall silent, A weary victory, with emotions violent. Freedom won, at a heavy cost, Ghosts of battles, forever embossed.

1. A Nation Rises

From thirteen colonies, a phoenix takes flight, With tattered wings, soaring into the light. A beacon of hope, a testament bold, A story of freedom, forever told.